Caroline Wightman

Sugar Gliders

Everything About Purchase,
Nutrition, Behavior,
and Breeding

BARRON'S

2 CONTENTS

PREFACE

Sugar gliders have become an indispensable part of my life. My husband claims that my interest in them could be more accurately described as an obsession.

My first pair of sugar gliders were not tame, but I found them intriguing nonetheless. They would not allow me to pick them up but they would consent to being stroked while they sat on a branch and they would take a favorite treat from my hand. I spent many hours just watching them and marveling at the dexterous way they handled their food and daintily groomed their fur. They checked out every corner of their cage with such bright-eyed curiosity, their ears rotating back and forth like radar dishes to pick up the smallest sounds.

Several months after I got my gliders, I noticed that the female had babies in her pouch. Then, I opened the nesting box one day to find the babies out of the pouch and curled up next to their mother. Their eyes were still shut and their fur was very short, but they were already adorable. Ten days later, their eyes opened and I started to handle them every day.

I couldn't believe how trusting the babies were. They loved being held and never once attempted to bite me. As they got older, they would ride on my shoulder or at the back of my neck or, if they needed a better view, the top of my head.

As time went on, they became more adventurous and would leave me for short excursions of exploration, making forays down the back of the sofa, but always returning to me periodically to check that I was still there.

It is hardly surprising that sugar gliders are becoming popular as pets in North America, Europe, and Japan. In addition to their obvious attractiveness and engaging personalities, they are easy to keep and can even be kept in an apartment. A sugar glider's diet and housing requirements are not difficult to cater to. They are not smelly and are very quiet the majority of the time. However, sugar gliders are not for everyone. They require a considerable investment in time and energy and a firm commitment to their consistent care.

I hope this book will help you decide whether or not a sugar glider is compatible with your lifestyle. If you do bring home a sugar glider, this book will assist you in giving your pet the best care and, in so doing, enhance your mutual enjoyment of one another.

MEET THE SUGAR GLIDER

Class: Mammalia
Subclass: Marsupialia
Order: Diprotodontia
Suborder: Phalangerida
Superfamily: Petauroidea
Family: Petauridae

What Is a Sugar Glider?

A sugar glider is a small marsupial possum found in the tree tops of Australia, Tasmania, Indonesia, and Papua-New Guinea. The sugar gliders are so named because they have a preference for sweet foods and a gliding membrane similar to that of a flying squirrel.

Taxonomic Classification

Taxonomic names are often designed to offer a description of an animal's physical attributes or behavioral traits. The sugar glider's specific taxonomic name, which is comprised of the genus and the species, is *Petaurus breviceps*. The genus, *Petaurus*, means "tightrope walker" or "rope dancer." The species name, *breviceps*, means "short head." Sugar

Sugar gliders are adept climbers
and acrobats.

gliders belong to a group of animals called phalangers, which means "fingery-one."

The Petauridae Family

Within the family Petauridae there are eleven species of possums split into three genera:

six species of *Petaurus*, which includes the sugar glider.

one species of *Gymnobelideus*, called Leadbeater's possum.

four species of *Dactylopsila*, the striped possums.

Not all members of the family Petauridae can glide. The striped possums and Leadbeater's possum do not have a gliding membrane. Conversely, there are possums that do not belong to the family Petauridae that *can* glide. Examples of these are the feathertail glider and the greater glider.

In addition to the Petauridae, there are five other families of possums: Pseudocheiridae (ringtail possums and greater gliders); Phalangeridae (brushtail possums and cuscuses); Acrobatidae (feathertail gliders); Burramyidae (pygmy possums); and Tarsipedidae (honey possums).

Sugar gliders are quite common. They are considered a secure species. Unfortunately, this is not true of the entire Petauridae family. Leadbeater's possum, the Mahogany glider, and the striped possum called Tate's Triok, are all considered endangered mainly due to loss of habitat. At one time, Leadbeater's possum was thought to be extinct until it was rediscovered in an area of Australia called the Victoria central highlands. The state of Victoria has adopted this prodigal possum as its faunal emblem.

Possum or Opossum?

Contrary to popular belief, the terms *possum* and *opossum* are not interchangeable. To refer to an American opossum as a *possum* is to abbreviate its real name. To refer to an Australian possum as an *opossum* is outdated and incorrect. The *o* has been dropped from the Australian possum's name in order to make a distinction between two very different groups of marsupials.

Captain James Cook's botanist, Sir Joseph Banks, is largely responsible for initiating the confusion. In 1770, while on a voyage to the South Pacific, Captain Cook and his crew spent time aground in Australia in an area that is now called Endeavour River (after Captain Cook's vessel, *The Endeavour*). While aground, Sir Joseph recorded the finding of "an animal of the Opossum tribe." This animal was in fact a common ringtail possum, and interestingly

Sugar gliders and their relatives are referred to as possums. American marsupials are referred to as opossums.

enough it still exists today (stuffed of course) in the Netherlands' natural history museum at Leyden. Sir Joseph probably chose the term *opossum* to describe the Australian animal because it was a marsupial and showed some resemblance to the marsupial opossums that he had observed in the Americas. It was an unfortunate choice on his part because the American and Australian marsupials are only distantly related and are very different from one another. It is a pity that Sir Joseph did not stay true to form and ask the aborigines what they called the animal (as he did with the kangaroo). If he had, possums would now be called "toolahs" or "bobucks" or something else uniquely Australian instead of the modified, secondhand American name they have today.

Subclass Marsupialia: The Marsupials

Sugar gliders belong in a subclass of mammals called marsupials. The marsupials comprise a diverse group of animals, with highly specialized adaptations for the wide spectrum of their lifestyles and environments. Marsupials can be found grazing on open savannas (wallabies and kangaroos), browsing on leaves in the tree tops (koalas), gliding through the trees in search of insects and nectar (sugar gliders), and living in burrows in the ground (wombats).

How Are Marsupials Different from Other Mammals?

Contrary to popular belief, it is not merely the possession of a pouch or *marsupium* that defines the marsupial. In fact, some marsupials do not have a pouch at all. Depending on the species, the pouch can vary greatly in size, depth, orientation of its opening, and the number and arrangement of the nipples found within. Marsupials are truly set apart from the rest of the mammals by their means of reproduction.

Marsupial Reproduction

Mammals are described as warm blooded, fur bearing animals that suckle their young with milk. Mammals that gestate their young placentally are called eutherian or placental mammals. The placenta is an organ that forms within the uterus during pregnancy. It facilitates the transfer of nutrients from the mother to the developing embryo. The vast majority of mammals, including humans, are placental mammals. Marsupials differ in that there is little or no emphasis on placentally gestating their young because, depending on the species, they have only rudimentary placentas, or none at all.

Marsupial offspring are born after a very short gestation. As a result, newborn marsupials are poorly developed and extremely tiny in relation to their parents. For example, an Eastern gray kangaroo weighing 66 pounds (30 kilograms) gives birth after a gestation of only 36 days to a baby weighing only .03 ounce (.8 gram).

Once inside the pouch, the baby marsupial, which is now referred to as a "joey," finds a mammary gland, and sucks it into its mouth. Its subsequent development is supported exclusively by lactation. By the time the joey is ready to emerge from the pouch, it is at a stage of development similar to that of some placentally gestated mammals at birth.

CHARACTERISTICS OF SUGAR GLIDERS

Sugar gliders live between five and seven years in the wild and twelve and fifteen years in captivity.

General Appearance

An adult sugar glider's head and body together measure about 5 to 6 inches (12.7–15.2 cm) with a tail of equal length. Sugar gliders are gray with a cream colored underside. A black stripe runs the full length of the back in line with the spine. It extends up and over the top of the head, terminating between the eyes. The last couple of inches on the tail are also black.

The Tail

The tail is not prehensile, in that it is not used for grasping, but is used as a tool for balancing and stabilizing. During a glide, the tail is used as a rudder to control the direction of flight.

A sugar glider's sharp claws help it to grip branches, which is especially important for landing after a glide.

Facial Features

The ears are fairly large and hairless and are constantly in motion, moving independently of one another like radar dishes in order to pick up the smallest sounds. Like most nocturnal animals, the eyes are large and protruding and set on the side of the face to allow for a wider field of vision.

Feet

Sugar gliders have five digits on each forefoot. Each digit terminates in an extremely sharp, scimitar shaped claw that is used for gripping during landing impact. The hind feet also have five digits, including an enlarged, clawless, opposable big toe. The second and third digits on the hind feet are interesting in that they are partially fused together (syndactylous) to form a grooming comb. Syndactylous toes can be seen in quite a few marsupials, including the wallabies and kangaroos.

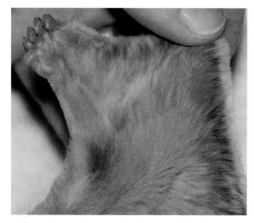

A furred membrane of skin stretches from the wrists to the ankles.

Gliding Membrane

A furred membrane of skin, called a *patagium*, stretches from the wrists to the ankles. When the glider is at rest, this excess skin appears as a rippled border along the animal's sides. During a glide, the skin is spread out to

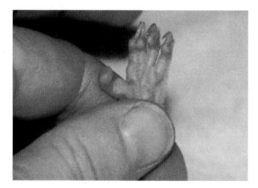

The hind feet have an enlarged, clawless, opposable big toe. The second and third digits are partially fused together to form a grooming comb.

form a rectangle, literally transforming the animal into a living kite.

The Skeleton

While it is true that sugar gliders superficially resemble flying squirrels, the similarity is only skin deep. Marsupial brains and skulls still have many reptilian characteristics. Marsupial pelvises differ from those of placental mammals in that there are usually two bones, called the epipubic bones, or marsupial bones, that branch off of the pelvis like a pair of abdominal ribs. It is thought that these bones serve to support the pouch area. However, it has recently been discovered that the epipubic bones are vestigial in sugar gliders and thus are not readily apparent.

Teeth

Marsupials have many more teeth than placental mammals. Sugar gliders are diprodonts—animals that have only two lower incisors that are large and forward pointing.

Body Temperature

In general, marsupials have a lower body temperature than placental mammals. A sugar glider's body temperature is 89°F (35°C). By comparison, a human's body temperature is 98.6°F (37°C) and a cat's is 102.2°F (39°C).

Body Weight

According to Strahan (1995), adult males range between 4.0 and 5.5 ounces (115–160 grams) in weight. An average male weighs approximately 5 ounces (140 grams). Females

range between 3.35 and 4.8 ounces (95–135 grams), for an average of 4 ounces (115 grams).

It is interesting that wild populations of sugar gliders from warmer climates are smaller than those from colder ones, and so one tends to see an increase in weight as their distance from the equator increases. Large sugar gliders are better adapted to colder temperatures than their smaller equatorial counterparts because large gliders lose heat at a slower pace than small ones.

Intelligence

Intelligence in animals is a difficult thing to quantify. Different species of equal intelligence may react quite differently to the same situation.

At one time, it was believed that marsupials were an inferior type of mammal and that they were lower on the evolutionary totem pole than placentals. In this scenario, it logically followed that marsupials were of inferior intelligence to placentals. A more recent view is that while marsupials and placentals are obviously different in a number of ways, one is not necessarily superior to the other. A wallaby is of similar intelligence to its placental counterpart, a deer. A sugar glider is, at the very least, as intelligent as a squirrel.

Sugar gliders are quite capable of recognizing the people that handle them regularly, which demonstrates that they have a memory. They can be trained to swoop down from a perch to a human shoulder on command. Sugar gliders can express affection, as well as displeasure when frightened or unhappy, by vocalizations and body language. Their imaginative play is a testament to their intellect.

IS A SUGAR GLIDER THE RIGHT PET FOR YOU?

If you buy a hand-tamed youngster you can expect it to form a strong and lifelong bond with you. However, do carefully consider whether you can consistently provide the kind of care a glider needs before you buy one.

Think Before You Buy a Sugar Glider

When given the right kind of care and attention, sugar gliders can be highly interactive, genuinely enjoyable pets. Too many people acquire pets on impulse without really considering the consequences to themselves or to the animals. Before you buy, carefully consider these questions:

• A sugar glider may live up to fifteen years in captivity. Are you prepared to be responsible for it for that long?

• Can you provide and outfit a reasonably large cage?

• Do you have the time and the inclination to clean cages and chop fresh fruit every day?

Sugar gliders live a long time and need a lot of attention.

• Sugar gliders are social animals. If you cannot afford to buy two to keep each other company, will you consistently take your pet out and handle it?

• If the sugar glider is intended for a child, are you prepared to supervise and participate in its care and handling?

• Have you thought about who will take care of your pet when you go away?

• Not every veterinarian treats exotic animals. Do you have a veterinarian who is willing to treat sugar gliders? And can you afford the bill if your pet requires medical attention?

• Do you have other pets in the house that might not adapt to living with sugar gliders?

• Are you, or any member of your family, allergic to animal fur?

• Will your landlord allow you to keep such an animal?

• Is your spouse going to divorce you if you bring home another pet?!

CONSIDERATIONS BEFORE YOU BUY

Now that you have decided that a sugar glider is the right pet for you, there are a few choices for you to make about the specific animal to purchase.

Would you prefer a male or a female? One sugar glider, a pair, or a group? You must also decide where you are going to make your purchase and ascertain that the supplier is reputable, knowledgeable, and able to provide you with a healthy pet.

State and Municipal Regulations

Prior to making any purchases, check with your state fish and wildlife department to confirm that it is permissible for you to have a sugar glider as a pet in your state. The fish and wildlife departments follow state guidelines, not federal. Therefore, what may be legal as a pet in one state may not be legal in another.

Make sure that gliders are permissible as pets where you live.

Community bylaws should also be checked to make sure that there are no local ordinances prohibiting certain exotics within your county. It is unlikely that there will be any bylaws prohibiting the ownership of something as inoffensive as a sugar glider, but it is always better to be safe than sorry.

Remember to confirm that your landlord or tenants' association has no objection to your prospective pet.

A Male or a Female?

Before you buy your pet, decide if you have a preference as to its gender. Breeders and pet owners differ in their opinions as to which gender makes the better pet. While sugar gliders do vary in personality from individual to individual, I have not noticed a link between behavior and gender. Both sexes seem to be equally hardy and to have the same life span in captivity.

reduce the possibility of excessive scent marking by having him neutered prior to the onset of sexual maturity.

I suggest that you assess a sugar glider's suitability as a pet on an individual basis. In the end, your decision is more likely to be dictated by the intangibles of love than the specifics of gender.

How Many Gliders?

Sugar gliders are social animals. If you can afford to buy more than one, do so. This will ensure that they have company and some stimulation outside of human interaction. If you go away on vacation or are too busy to handle them consistently, they will be less affected if they have the companionship of their own kind. It is not necessary to keep gliders in gender pairs. Two males or two females will get along just as well as a male and a female.

Finding Suppliers

Sugar gliders are advertised for sale in local newspapers, exotic pet magazines, and on bulletin boards in veterinarians' offices. While many pet stores don't stock sugar gliders because of their nocturnal nature, they may be able to help you find a breeder in your area. You might be able to find sugar gliders at a local pet fair or an exotic animal auction. If you are considering buying an animal at an auction, use extreme caution. Some disreputable breeders and dealers use auctions as a means of anonymously disposing of old, sick, and barren animals. Many of the lots have no identifying labels on them to tell you who the seller is, and little or no information is provided regarding

It is true that male gliders have several more scent glands than the females but they are not overly smelly. The males occasionally give off a short burst of fruity, musky scent (usually when they are awakened), but it is not strong, and doesn't last long. It is not the kind of musky odor one associates with skunks or ferrets and it does not permeate a room.

Having said that, though, I have heard reports of male gliders that are unusually enthusiastic about scent marking their cage and this can be problematic from an odor perspective. If you have your heart set on a male, and you don't intend to breed him, it is possible to the animal's care requirements. While you will probably pay less than retail, you may find that you get less than a bargain in the end.

Choosing a Supplier

If possible, acquire your sugar glider locally because shipping is always stressful for an animal (and the recipient of the animal when they see the bill). If you buy locally, you will have the advantage of being able to see, firsthand, the kind of facility in which your glider was raised. If you have any questions or concerns, a local supplier is more accessible than one across the country. However, buying locally is less important than buying from a caring, reputable, and knowledgeable source. If you are able to find a supplier nearby, go and look at the facilities to ascertain that the animals are being adequately housed and fed and that the premises are clean. Ask:

• How long have they been in business?
• Do they possess all the required licensing to breed or sell gliders?
• Can they provide references?
• How knowledgeable are they about the animals they are selling?

• Will they make themselves available to answer your questions regarding your new pet once you have purchased it and taken it home?
• What kind of guarantee does the animal come with concerning its health and breeding ability?

Check the references that the seller provides you with to see if past customers are happy with their animals and that they received all the after-sale help they needed. Obtain in writing any guarantees that the seller is willing to provide you with. Make sure the written document outlines your purchase agreement in detail so that there can be no misunderstandings about what was intended.

You can expect responsible suppliers to ask a number of questions of *you*. They will want to know why specifically you have chosen a glider and if you are aware of the level of commitment that is involved with its care. Responsible suppliers do not sell to those who appear to be buying on impulse, to those who don't seem to be interested in learning about the animal's care requirements, or to those who are motivated to buy an unusual pet because they think it will gain them attention.

PET SELECTION

Now that you have learned that it's permissible for you to own sugar gliders in the area that you live in, and you've decided from whom you are going to purchase your glider, whether you would prefer a male or a female, and how many gliders you're going to buy, you're ready to select your pet.

What Age?

It's best to pick out a recently weaned animal as it will bond with you more readily. However, don't choose one that is so young that it is not eating easily on its own. The eyes should have been open for between a month to six weeks at the time of purchase. The tail should be fluffy, like an adult's. If the tail is covered with short, smooth hairs that conform to the shape of the tail, it indicates that the animal has been out of the pouch for less than three weeks and it is not ready to be weaned. It is also possible for a glider to be too old to make a good pet. The glider doesn't have to be too far past the baby stage for this to happen. Don't buy an animal that is not already tame if you are inexperienced with gliders. It's generally not a good idea to take the breeder's or pet store owner's word for it that the animal is still young enough to settle down with handling.

The age of a glider can be a confusing issue because some sellers base the age on the approximate time that the animal was born, while other sellers choose to calculate the age from its emergence from the pouch. When a sugar glider's eyes have been open for a month it is approximately 12 to 13 weeks old, based on its birth date. However, it has only been out of the pouch for four to five weeks. When asking the age of a sugar glider, it is best to have the sellers clarify which system they are using to measure age.

Selecting a Healthy and Suitable Pet

When selecting your sugar glider, look for the following:
• Bright, clear eyes that are free of cataracts, white spots, and discharge.
• A reasonably fleshed appearance. The pelvic bones should not be overly apparent.

• Fur that is soft, thick, and clean.
• Properly formed stools. The stools should look like moist mouse droppings. If there is caked feces on the fur at the base of the tail, it is an indication that the animal may have diarrhea.
• An active and alert attitude. Observe your prospective pet in its cage. It should move freely across the wire and its branches. An animal that sits apathetically in a corner or that has difficulty moving around is probably ill.
• A friendly and curious nature. Have the seller remove the sugar glider from its cage and handle it for you (if anyone's going to get bitten, it might as well be him). He will demonstrate the correct way to pick the glider up and hold it. The glider should be content to stay on the person handling it. It should not keep jumping off and running away. When the sugar glider is passed to you for handling, it will be a little hesitant at first because it is not used to your scent, but it should be reasonably friendly and interested in checking you out. If the sugar glider passes this inspection then, in all probability, it is a healthy and suitable pet.

Don't be tempted to buy a sick or neglected animal simply because you feel that it needs rescuing. People who purchase such animals usually find themselves with an unfriendly, sickly pet, that requires the costly services of

a veterinarian to correct its health problems. It is only natural to want to remove an animal from a bad situation, but the effort, while well meaning, is counterproductive because it allows those people who engage in poor breeding and husbandry practices to profit by the inferior or indifferent management of their animals. Unfortunately, the purchase of such animals only finances the next crop of the sickly and the neglected.

If you feel strongly that an animal's situation is unacceptable, contact your local Society for the Prevention of Cruelty to Animals (SPCA), the Humane Society, or the United States Department of Agriculture (USDA), which oversees the licensing of those who breed and sell animals.

It is important to have a suitable cage and all the equipment you will need to care for your new pet prior to bringing it home.

Size of the Cage

People often ask me how big a cage for a sugar glider should be. Some of my cages containing colonies of gliders are four feet deep by eight feet long by seven feet high and could more accurately be described as aviaries. However, they would not fit too well into most living rooms. The cage should be as big as you can practically manage while being no smaller than 20 × 20 × 30 inches high (50.8 × 50.8 × 76.2 cm). This size of cage is adequate for one or two gliders. If the cage is a few inches smaller than 20 inches (50.8 cm) at the base, but a few inches taller than 30 inches (76.2 cm) high, it amounts to the same thing. A tall cage is better than a long squat one because sugar gliders like to climb. Commercial bird cages often meet these specifications.

The wire of the cage should be no bigger than 1 inch by $1/2$ inch (2.5 × 1.25 cm). If the cage is to have straight bars with no cross-

hatching, then the bars should be no more than a $1/4$ inch (6.25 mm) apart. These are referred to in pet stores as "budgie bars." Don't use screen door mesh to build a homemade cage because the gliders have a tendency to get their claws caught in it.

Some of my larger cages have wire only on the front and the rest is constructed of plywood. I have never had a problem with the sugar gliders trying to chew their way out but then we have been very careful not to leave any edges exposed that might tempt them. The sugar glider's claws provide them with such a sure grip that I have seen them appear to defy gravity by walking across a vertical piece of plywood. If you decide to build a cage and paint it, make sure that you use a nontoxic, lead-free paint. A nontoxic, high gloss latex or melamine paint is durable, washable, and easy to keep clean. Be sure to allow the correct interval for drying and curing of the paint.

It is not safe to place an animal in a newly painted cage until the paint is completely cured.

Cleaning Considerations

The only drawback I have found to building my own cages is that $1 \times \frac{1}{2}$ inch (2.5 × 1.25 cm) galvanized wire is harder to clean than the enameled, straight bars of a commercial cage. Sugar gliders often urinate while they are clinging to the wire and the urine will gradually build up as a whitish deposit on the mesh unless it is cleaned off regularly. Commercial cages also have the advantage of a slide-out plastic tray, which makes cleaning easy and convenient.

Make sure the door on the cage is big enough to allow passage of the nesting box. If you need to remove your gliders from the cage to do a thorough cleaning, you can simply remove the nesting box, complete with its sleeping residents, to another container. This is especially important if you do not have tame animals. Catching unfriendly gliders individually can be both time-consuming and traumatic to the fingers, and can increase the opportunities for escape. It is also a stressful experience for the glider.

If your cage is small enough to fit, the best place to clean it is in a bathtub or shower stall, where it can be scrubbed and rinsed with ease. Be careful not to leave any soap or detergent residue on the bars where it might be licked off.

Location of the Cage

Most keep their pet gliders in the house year-round, but depending on the seasonal temperature and the kind of facilities you have, gliders can also be kept in a screened-in porch or in a heated outbuilding. I have seen sugar gliders kept in outdoor aviaries, during the summer months, as far north as southern Washington state, but personally I worry about them being menaced by wandering cats, dogs, and birds of prey. Obviously, if they escape from an outdoor aviary, the chances of recovering them are remote.

When choosing a place to put your sugar glider's enclosure, select a place that is not frequented by a flow of noisy human traffic during the day so that your slumbering pet will not be constantly disturbed.

If the cage is not of the floor-to-ceiling variety, it should be placed up on a table or countertop because gliders like the sensation of height. However, do not place the cage on top of appliances such as refrigerators or television sets, which emit a constant low grade noise and vibration that some sensitive animals find disturbing.

Place the cage in a location that gets enough light so that there is a notable difference between night and day, *but not in direct sunlight* as this can be damaging to a sugar glider's nocturnal eyes. Overexposure to sunlight has been known to cause retinal cancer in some nocturnal animals. In addition, nesting boxes may become too hot for comfort if placed in direct sunlight.

Sugar gliders come from areas of the world that are equatorial. In their natural environment there is very little seasonal variation in the length of the days and nights. Sugar gliders that are kept in basements or windowless rooms will suffer from stress because their biological clocks become confused when there is no light/dark interval to cue them to sleep, exercise, or feed. Where natural light is not available, a light on a timer should be provided. Keep in mind that some exposure to ultraviolet light is necessary for manufacturing vitamin D.

Temperature

Sugar gliders should be kept at between 65°F (18°C) and 75°F (24°C). This is very convenient because it is the room temperature range commonly found in most homes.

Inside the Cage

Nesting Boxes

Sugar gliders are nocturnal and need a place to curl up and go to sleep during the day. A nesting box will provide your pet with a hiding place where it can feel safe and protected while it slumbers. Nesting boxes can be made out of wood, wicker, or plastic. Alternatively, a cloth pouch with a slit in the front can be tied to the side of the cage as a sleeping bag. Gliders like to "move house" occasionally and so it is a good idea to provide several types of nesting boxes in the same cage.

A wooden birdhouse makes an ideal bedroom, as does a plastic hamster house or a rubber storage container that has an entrance hole and ventilation holes cut in it. The entrance hole should be no smaller than $1^1/2$ inches (3.75 cm) in diameter. Female gliders that have large babies in their pouch, or youngsters clinging to their back or underside, will find it difficult to get in and out if the hole is any smaller. If the nesting box is for a breeding pair, it is advantageous if the entrance hole is high up on one of the sides or in the lid so that the babies cannot inadvertently fall out. Nesting boxes that have

removable or hinged lids are best because they provide better access to sleeping pets and are easier to clean. The nesting box should be placed as high up in the cage as possible because sugar gliders do not feel secure sleeping near the floor.

Bedding

Sugar gliders will quite happily sleep in nesting boxes or sleeping bags that contain no bedding. However, you can add plain shredded paper or pine or aspen wood shavings. Aspen is preferable to pine because it does not contain volatile resins or other terpenoids. Alternatively, a piece of cloth or a sock can be provided for the glider to curl up in. Wood shavings or plain paper can also be used in the bottom of the cage to catch and absorb moisture from urine, droppings, and fruit that has fallen from the dishes.

Don't use newspaper or magazine paper because it may contain harmful dyes and chemicals. Do not use cedar shavings or make nesting boxes out of cedar. Cedar contains volatile compounds that are harmful and can cause respiratory problems to some animals.

In rare instances, a sugar glider may try to consume inedible bedding. This behavior is most often seen in young gliders that are given bedding materials that they are not familiar with. They attempt to eat the substance out of inexperience. However, consumption of inedible material can also be a sign of nutritional deficiency.

If your sugar glider appears to be eating its bedding or shavings from the bottom of the cage, remove the substance immediately because the glider's digestive system may become impacted by these materials. It will be necessary to find alternative bedding and cage floor material. For example, paper towels can be used instead of wood shavings.

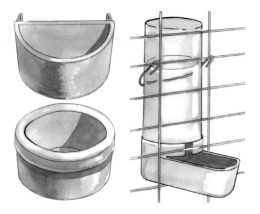

A variety of receptacles can be used to dispense your glider's food and water.

Litter Box?

Sugar gliders will not use a litter box. They cannot be house trained. However, they are quite clean animals that usually avoid soiling their nesting box. They do not produce copious amounts of stools and urine. Stools are like those of a mouse and quickly dry to a hard pellet. They usually urinate while on the wire or on the branches in their cage.

To avoid having your glider urinate or defecate on you when you take it out, gently brush the area at the base of the tail with a piece of toilet tissue. This will stimulate the glider to soil the toilet tissue rather than you or your furnishings.

Food and Water Containers

Food can be placed in a variety of receptacles from flat-bottomed, non-tip dishes to bird dishes that clip onto the wire. Water can also be dispensed from a non-tip dish, a clip-on bird dish, or a sipper-type water bottle. If you choose to use a water bottle (which is best because the glider cannot foul its water with stools or urine), it is important to also supply a dish of water until you are sure that your glider has located the water bottle and has learned how to drink from it. Flat-bottomed, glass ashtrays make good water dishes because they are shallow and too heavy for a glider to tip over.

It is important that the dishes and bottles containing food, juice, or water be sanitized daily to prevent the build-up of harmful bacteria.

Food and water should be placed high up in the cage because this is where sugar gliders feed the most comfortably.

Climbing Branches

The addition of branches to a sugar glider's cage makes its environment more stimulating

and provides a more natural habitat. Make sure that you use a nontoxic species of wood. In general, if a type of wood is rated as safe for small birds, it is safe for sugar gliders. I have successfully used apple wood, aspen, cotton-wood, and willow. Use live or winter-dormant wood. The leaves can be left attached to the boughs, if so desired, because sugar gliders will sometimes amuse themselves by stripping off

the leaves and taking them back to their nest to be used as bedding.

Do not use the branches from coniferous trees such as pine, cedar, fir, and redwood that produce a sticky, resinous sap. Sugar gliders will sometimes strip the bark from their branches and the resins can get stuck in their fur.

Thoroughly rinse any boughs that may have been sprayed with chemicals in order to remove

all residues of pesticides before you place them in the cage.

Once your gliders have stripped the bark from their climbing branches, or the branches have become soiled, replace them with new ones.

Toys

Sugar gliders enjoy playing with bird toys such as swings, perches, ladders, and bells. Make sure that the toy is well put together and does not have small pieces that can be pulled off and swallowed. A piece of hard bone makes a good chew toy and it's good for their teeth, but do not use bird bones, which splinter easily, or greasy pork or lamb bones. Gliders like to play in things that they can climb through, explore, and hide in. A piece of PVC pipe makes a handy, washable hiding place.

Sugar gliders enjoy playing in clear plastic exercise balls.

I do not recommend using the wire hamster's wheels commonly found in most pet stores because, over the years, I have seen them injure too many animals. They are especially hazardous if there are several animals in the cage because while one animal is running in the wheel, others can get their appendages caught in the moving parts. There is a safe version of an exercise wheel that has been designed to eliminate the possibility of these types of injuries occurring. These safe wheels are completely enclosed on the back and there are no gaps into which a limb or tail can slip. This is the only type of wheel that I let my gliders play in. It is also possible to order sandpaper strips that fit inside the wheel. These inserts provide additional traction and are cleverly designed to protect the sensitive pads of the glider's feet while exposing the sharp ends of its claws to the abrasive undersurface. A pedicure and cardio workout all in one!

Some gliders enjoy playing in clear plastic exercise balls, but they shouldn't be allowed to play in these near the top of stairs or on landings where they might roll off. The exercise balls also come with a stand that the ball can rotate in.

An acquaintance told me about her male glider's exploits in an exercise ball. Apparently, he realizes that he is protected within the ball's plastic shell because it is only then that he presumes to chase the family cat!

Sugar gliders like to climb, so a small cage should be taller than it is wide. If you decide to build a very large cage, use a wood or metal frame on which to attach the cage wire. Wood surfaces can be painted with a washable nontoxic paint. Do not leave any small holes or edges exposed in the wood because the gliders may be encouraged to enlarge holes and chew edges. Smaller wire cages do not require a frame because they can be joined together using J-clips. The cage in this example is 22 × 22 × 30 inches (56 × 56 × 76 cm) high and is suitable for one or two gliders. However, keep in mind that a glider's cage can never be too large. If you have the space and the finances to build a bigger cage, then do so. For the cage

in this example you will need:
• 13 feet (4 m) of 1 × $\frac{1}{2}$ inch (2.5 × 1.25 cm) galvanized wire, 30 inches (76 cm) wide.
• 1 metal, plastic, or wood tray that is slightly smaller than the cage if it is to fit inside the cage or slightly larger if the cage is to sit inside the tray.
• side-cutting wire cutting pliers or shears
• J-clip pliers and J-clips
• hot-melt glue gun and glue sticks
• measuring tape
• 1 length of plastic trim (sold as paneling end-capping in eight foot lengths; available in a variety of colors)
• 1 piece of 10 gauge galvanized strand wire, 12 inches (30.5 cm) long. This will be fashioned into the door catch.

The preceding materials and tools can be purchased from

hardware stores and agricultural suppliers. Plastic or metal trays can be purchased from plastic or steel fabricators.

Cut the cage wire into six panels that are 22 inches long and as wide as the roll. Take two of the panels and trim them so that they are 22 × 22 inches (56 × 56 cm). These will be the top and the bottom of the cage. The trim from the top and the bottom panels will be used as shelves. If your cage is to have an inside sliding tray, you will need to cut a piece off of the 22 × 30 inch (56 × 76 cm) front panel to allow for the passage of the tray. The amount you cut off the bottom of the front panel should correspond to the depth of your tray.

Join the panels that form the front, back, and sides of the cage, using the J-clips and the J-clip pliers. Attach the floor next. Do not attach the top until you have installed the two (or more) shelves. It is best to attach the shelves so that one is above the other at right angles to each other. This gives the cage additional strength and reinforcement. If you attach the back of the shelf so that it is slightly lower than the front and curl the front of the shelf up

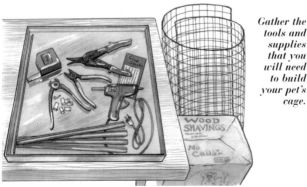

Gather the tools and supplies that you will need to build your pet's cage.

slightly, you will find that objects such as food bowls and nesting boxes are less likely to fall off. Attach the top of the cage next.

Cut a square doorway in the front panel of the cage that is 10 × 10 inches (25.5 × 25.5 cm). Place the doorway in the middle of the front panel about 10 inches (25.5 cm) from the top of the cage. This will provide good access to the interior of the cage. Cut the door so that it is 11 × 11 inches (28 × 28 cm). Attach the door to the cage, 1 inch (2.5 cm) back from the edge of the doorway so that you will be able to attach your plastic trim around the doorway without having to leave spaces for the hinges. The door is attached to the cage using two or three J-clips as hinges.

Using the hot melt glue gun, run a generous amount of glue into the groove in the back of the plastic trim. Place the trim over any sharp edges that could injure a sugar glider (or a person inserting an arm into the cage).

To make the door catch, bend your 12 inches (30.5 cm) of 10 gauge strand wire into the configuration illustrated above. (Alternatively, it is sometimes possible to purchase wire that has been pre-bent to these specifications from steel fabricators and cage manufacturers.) Attach the catch to the door using the J-clips. Close the door to see where the catch lines up with the cage wire and then crimp the wire together at that location in order to allow for easy passage of the catch.

Place the tray in or under your creation as desired and you have a cage. Add a nesting box or two, toys, branches, food bowls and water containers, and, of course, a sugar glider or two.

Heavy–Metal Toxicity

Galvanized wire has been known to cause heavy-metal (zinc, antimony, arsenic, etc.) toxi-

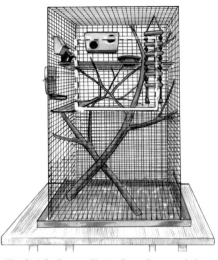

The finished cage. Notice how the two shelves have been positioned at right angles to each other in order to provide additional strength to the structure.

city in animals and birds that chew on or habitually lick the wire of their cage. While I have never heard of a case of heavy-metal toxicity in sugar gliders, it is advisable to wash a newly constructed cage to remove any loose particles of metal. Most authorities recommend washing fresh galvanized metal with white vinegar and then rinsing thoroughly. Never place your gliders' food directly on a galvanized metal surface because their diet is on the acidic side and heavy-metal residues can leach into their food.

There are plastic-coated, welded-wire hardware products available in some hardware stores. The plastic-coated wire is superior to galvanized wire because the possibility for heavy-metal toxicity is eliminated, and there is also less possibility of trauma to an animal's feet from sharp edges. Unfortunately, this product can be quite difficult to find.

LIVING WITH SUGAR GLIDERS

Be patient with your new pet. Don't be surprised if it makes disgruntled noises at you to begin with when you try to handle it. Gliders need time to learn a new person's scent.

Bringing Your Pet Home

Finally, you get to bring your new pet home. Don't give in to your eagerness to handle your pet on the way home and open the crate. I know an unfortunate man who spent four hours taking the instrument panel of his van apart after his newly acquired sugar glider (which was understandably upset and disoriented in its new surroundings) decided to hide behind the dashboard.

When you arrive home, slide the container into the cage, open it, and let the glider come out in its own good time. Don't invite all the neighbors over to admire your new treasure. Your pet will need time to settle in and is bound to be a little apprehensive for the first day or so.

Your new glider may be shy at first and reluctant to come out of the nesting box or pouch.

It is a good idea to place a couple of pieces of fruit inside the nesting box in case your new friend is too shy to come out at first. Choose nutritious, juicy fruits such as papaya and mango that will satisfy your new pet's thirst as well as its hunger. Add a piece of cloth that has been carried on your person to the nesting box so that the glider can become familiar with your scent. A clean handkerchief that has been carried close to the skin works well. The cloth should *not* be scented with cologne or perfume.

Handling Your Pet

After your new pet has had a day or so to settle in and check out its new surroundings, reach in and remove it gently from its nesting box. Do this during the day when it is sleepy and easier to handle. Put any other pets such as dogs, cats, ferrets, and large birds in another room because your glider might be frightened by their presence.

While it is not harmful to pick gliders up gently and briefly by lightly gripping the base of the tail, this should not be necessary with a tame one. *Never* pull on a glider's tail in order to extract it from its nesting box or pull it from wire or objects to which it is clinging. I have heard some horror stories about tails that have come off in people's hands. Pick your glider up bodily and hold it in your cupped hands or against your chest. If the glider resists being picked up by gripping objects in his cage, put your finger behind his claws and gently push them off of the object.

Once your glider has settled down, you can place it in your pocket where it will probably go back to sleep. Put your hand in the pocket and stroke your pet occasionally so that it will get used to your scent and being touched. Eventu-

ally, the glider will find the nerve to come out and explore a little. Let it climb up onto your shoulder and check you out. Don't be surprised if it wants to climb through your hair.

Letting Gliders Out to Play

I have a pair of tame gliders in a cage in my living room. At night, I open their cage door and they come out to play. Typically, they run up the curtains and survey the room from the curtain rod, check out the plants, do a few laps of the room, and then come and climb on me for a while. After a few hours of this, they return to their cage of their own volition.

A friend of mine has a glider that has discovered his stairwell. Its favorite game is to launch itself off the landing and glide to the bottom of the stairs, then it runs back up and repeats the procedure over and over again, just like a little kid going down a water slide.

Encouraging Your Pet to Glide to You

Once your pet has completely bonded with you and is comfortable in its surroundings, you can attempt to teach it to glide to you.

Place your pet in a location that is higher than your shoulder where it would have difficulty getting down by any other route than by jumping to you and climbing down. The top of a bookshelf might work. Place your glider on the shelf and show it a small treat. Place the treat in the palm of your hand and hold it up so that your glider has to step off of the shelf onto your hand to collect its reward. Repeat the

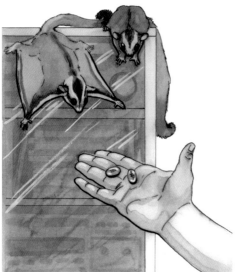

Encourage your glider to jump to you by showing it a treat in the palm of your hand and then moving your hand further away.

procedure but this time move your hand slightly further away from the edge of the shelf so that your glider has to make a very small leap to get to you. Increase the distance as your glider becomes more adept at the game.

Household Hazards

Gliders turned loose in a room can be extremely entertaining and interesting to watch, but *never* leave them unsupervised. It doesn't take long for a glider to escape through an open window or door, or an uncovered heating vent. Standing water in buckets, bathtubs, sinks, and toilets can make for a watery grave. Serious burns can be inflicted by hot stovetops, heat registers, and irons. Many house plants are poisonous and can cause illness and death if your pet is allowed to chew them (see Sugar Gliders and House Plants, page 39). Other potentially toxic substances are household cleansers, antifreeze, gasoline, oil, nail polish, nail polish remover, makeup, glue, ink, alcoholic and caffeinated drinks, drugs, dirty ashtrays, aerosol sprays such as hair spray, room deodorizer and perfume, and paint and varnish and their vapors.

In short, it will be necessary to childproof the area that your glider is allowed to play in. However, this does not preclude the need for supervision. If you don't know exactly where your pet is, it might get stepped on or sat on.

Handling Gliders During the Day

It is not harmful to wake up your sugar glider and handle it during the day, but after it has been handled for an hour or so it will start to look for a place to curl up and go back to sleep. If it wants to get into your pocket for a nap then let it do so. You do not want to stress

Gliders let loose in a room to play can be extremely entertaining to watch.

your pet by forcing it to stay up longer than it wants to. If you regularly handle your pet at a certain time of day, you might find that it will automatically start getting up at that time in anticipation of your visit.

Taking Gliders Outside

Don't take your glider outside until you are absolutely sure that it has bonded to you and is content to stay on your person. Don't take gliders outside in bright sunshine. Direct, bright light, is an unpleasant experience for a sugar glider and excessive exposure can lead to retinal damage.

Sugar gliders instinctively want to be as high up as possible so stay away from the trunks of trees or any other object that is tall enough to make retrieval difficult should your pet decide to seek refuge.

I have talked to some people that put a small harness and leash, of the type designed for reptiles, on their pet gliders when they take them outside. They like the extra measure of security that the harnesses provide. They assure me that these restraints are quite effective and don't seem to be distracting to the sugar glider or overly restrictive of its movements. However, they should not be relied upon too heavily as a means of control.

If you must take your glider outside and you are not absolutely sure that you can control it, place it inside a pet carrier or a container that can be securely fastened while still providing adequate ventilation.

Sugar Gliders and Other Pets

In the wild, the sugar glider's main predators are birds of prey such as owls. They should not be housed in the same room as screechy birds, such as cockatoos and parrots, because they find their calls threatening.

When it comes to dogs and cats, use discretion and caution. If your dog or cat couldn't care less about the presence of a sugar glider in a cage, then it shouldn't be a problem. If, how-ever, your canine or feline friend spends its time looking hungrily through the bars and drooling, then I would consider putting the cage somewhere out of reach. My Jack Russell terriers have been raised with so many different animals in the house that they know they are not allowed to act aggressively toward any animal, regardless of its diminutive size or the fact that it might insist on riding them around the room. However, these are exceptional dogs. I do not recommend that you trust your carnivorous pets with your sugar glider.

I have been asked on occasion if it is possible to keep sugar gliders and others animals such as flying squirrels in the same cage. *No.* They have different dietary requirements and, if they don't kill each other, they will find each other's presence in a confined space stressful. I heard about a man who tried to keep sugar gliders and finches in the same aviary. He doesn't have finches anymore but the sugar gliders are fatter and they have some nice feather lined nesting boxes.

There is nothing wrong with keeping sugar gliders, flying squirrels, hedgehogs, and so on in the same room as long as they are in separate cages.

I have successfully kept guinea pigs and rabbits in the bottom of my large aviaries because the sugar gliders are not interested in their food and rarely come down to the floor, and the guinea pigs and rabbits can't climb. However, keeping mixed species in the same cage is generally not recommended.

Sugar Gliders and Children

Sugar gliders are not a suitable pet for a child under age 12. Young children, in general,

Safe House Plants

Acacia	Figs: creeping, rubber,	Pittosporum
African Violet	fiddle leaf, laurel leaf,	Prayer plant
Aloe	weeping	Purple passion
Baby's tears	Monkey plant	Schefflera (umbrella)
Bamboo	Nasturtium	Sensitive plant
Begonia	Natal plum	Spider plant
Bougainvillea	Norfolk island pine	Swedish ivy
Chickweed	Palms: areca, date, fan, lady,	Thistle
Cissus	parlor, howeia, kentia,	Wandering Jew
Dracaena	Phoenix, sago	White clover
Ferns: asparagus,	Peperomia	Zebra plant
birds nest, Boston	Petunia	

Source: Adapted from *The Complete Bird Owners Handbook*, by Gary A. Gallerstein, DVM, and Heather Acker, AHT. New York: Howell Book House, 1994.

don't have the patience, gentleness, and sense of responsibility necessary to adequately look after gliders (mind you, this is also true of some 30 year olds I know). If you decide to buy a glider for a child, keep in mind that you are going to have to supervise its handling as well as its care.

Sugar Gliders and House Plants

Gliders just love to play in house plants, but this can be hard on the plants. Even if the glider does not chew the plant, repeatedly running through its foliage will produce wear and tear. It is a good idea to rotate the vegetation in your sugar glider's play area so that the plants have a chance to recover between thrashings.

Confirm that the house plants that your gliders have access to are all nontoxic varieties. If you have toxic plants, leave them in an area that your glider does not have access to. Do not allow your gliders to be near any plants that have been sprayed with pesticides.

The lists of safe and unsafe plants are not comprehensive but serve as a guide.

There are far too many potentially poisonous house plants, shrubs, and trees to list them all. Some plants and trees are considered generally poisonous while others are only dangerous if the seeds, pits, or fruit are consumed. If in doubt about the toxicity of a plant, consult your veterinarian or your local plant nursery.

Escapees

Because sugar gliders are active and curious, it won't take them long to find a fault in their cage if one exists. A broken weld on a bar or an improperly secured door will soon be discovered.

If your glider escapes, do the obvious: Close all the doors and windows, put the dog and the cat out of harm's way, and put the lid down on the

Poisonous Plants

Plant	Poisonous Parts
Amaryllis	Bulbs
American yew	Needles, seeds
Azalea	Leaves
Balsam pear	Seeds, rind of fruit
Baneberry	Berries, roots
Bird of paradise	Seeds
Black locust	Bark, sprouts, foliage
Blue-green algae	some forms toxic
Boxwood	Leaves, stems
Buckthorn	Fruit, bark
Buttercup	Sap, bulbs
Calla lily	Leaves
Caladium	Leaves
Castor bean (castor oil plant)	Beans, leaves
Chalice vine	All parts
Cherry tree	Bark, twigs, leaves, pits
Christmas cactus	All Parts
Christmas candle	Sap
Clematis	All parts
Coral plant	Seeds
Cowslip	All parts
Daffodil	Bulbs
Daphne	Berries
Datura	Berries
Deadly amanita	All parts
Death camas	All parts
Delphinium	All parts
Dieffenbachia	Leaves
Eggplant	All parts except fruit
Elephant's ear (taro)	Leaves, stem
English ivy	Berries, leaves
English yew	Needles, seeds
False Henbane	All parts
Foxglove	Leaves, seeds
Golden chain (laburnum)	All parts
Hemlock, poison and water	All parts
Henbane	Seeds
Holly	Berries
Horse chestnut	Nuts, twigs
Hyacinth	Bulbs
Hydrangea	Flower bud
Indian turnip (jack-in-the-pulpit)	All parts
Iris (blue flag)	Bulbs
Japanese yew	Needles, seeds

Plant	Poisonous Parts
Java bean (lima bean)	Uncooked beans
Jerusalem cherry	Berries
Jimsonweed (thornapple)	Leaves, seeds
Juniper	Needles, stems, berries
Lantana	Immature berries
Larkspur	All parts
Laurel	All parts
Lily-of-the-valley	All parts
Lobelia	All parts
Locoweed	All parts
Lords and Ladies (cucoopint)	All parts
Marijuana	Leaves
Mayapple	All parts, except fruit
Mescal bean	Seeds
Mistletoe	Berries
Mock orange	Fruit
Monkshood	Leaves, roots
Morning glory	All parts
Mother-in-law's tongue	All parts
Narcissus	Bulbs
Nightshades (all types)	Berries, leaves
Oleander	All parts
Philodendron	Leaves, stem
Poison ivy	Sap
Poison oak	Sap
Poinsettia	Leaves, flowers
Pokeweed (inkberry)	Leaves, roots, immature berries
Potato	Eyes, new shoots
Pothos	All Parts
Privet	All parts
Rhododendron	All parts
Rhubarb	Leaves
Rosary pea (Indian licorice)	Seeds
Skunk cabbage	All parts
Snowdrop	All parts
Snow-on-the-mountain	All parts
Sweet pea	Leaves
Tobacco	Leaves
Virginia creeper	Sap
Western yew	Needles, seeds
Wisteria	All parts
Yam bean	Roots, immature pods

Source: Adapted from *The Complete Bird Owner's Handbook,* by Gary A. Gallerstein, DVM, and Heather Acker, AHT. New York: Howell Book House, 1994.

If the cage is not completely secure, it will not take your glider long to make its escape.

toilet. I've heard a few terribly sad stories about escaped or poorly supervised sugar gliders that have drowned in toilet bowls. Do not remove anything from the house without checking it first. Check the trash can, if it doesn't have a lid, before you take it out. Check through your laundry before you put it in the washing machine. Look under seat cushions before you sit down, and check your shoes before you put them on. Before you go to bed, set some nesting boxes out with fruit inside them and hopefully you will find your glider sleeping in one when you get up in the morning.

Biting

Like all animals that have teeth, sugar gliders are capable of biting. However, this is not a common behavior of tame gliders. Even non-tame animals will usually only bite as a last

resort. Occasionally, a glider may go through a rebellious phase as it approaches sexual maturity and has a tendency to be nippy during this period. I have found that if I continue to handle such animals and ignore the biting, they will eventually stop this behavior.

If you are bitten by a tame glider it's probably because you are being too rough or holding it too tight. If you are a stranger to the glider, it may be frightened by your unfamiliar scent and it might bite out of fear.

Sugar gliders usually do not inflict the kind of dangerous, lacerating bites that require stitches. The bite will either be glancing and leave two minor parallel scratches or be a puncturing bite, much like being bitten by a hamster.

If you are bitten, take the usual precautions of washing and disinfecting the wound. If you have an adverse reaction or the wound becomes infected, consult a physician.

Sugar Gliders and Strangers

Be very cautious if you let someone that is strange to your glider handle it. Even if your pet is very tame and friendly with you, it might react quite violently to certain strangers. In addition, scared gliders have a habit of emptying their bladders and their bowels. Not only is it unfair to your pet to inflict such a frightening ordeal upon it, but you may also find yourself in an extremely embarrassing and upsetting situation if a visitor is bitten or has his clothing ruined.

Vacations

Gliders can be left alone for up to 24 hours, but beyond that you will need to find someone to come in and look after them. If you are

going to be gone overnight, make sure that your gliders have adequate food and water, and that their cage is clean prior to your departure.

Sugar gliders are not really the kind of animal you can take along on vacation. Gliders are creatures of habit. They like familiar surroundings and a predictable routine. Traveling can be a very stressful experience for a glider. On the trip it might get jostled around, chilled, overheated, suffer from motion sickness, and become frightened by all the strange smells and noises. Your pet will be much happier left at home with a competent caregiver.

Find your glider-sitter well in advance of leaving for your vacation. If possible, have the person come over to feed and spend time with the gliders in your home. If you must move your gliders and their cage over to the caretaker's home, do so at least several days prior to leaving on your vacation. Help the caretaker to glider proof the area where your pets will be allowed out for their evening exercise, and

spend time with the gliders in this area so that the transition will be smoother. Go through a couple of test runs with your helper prior to leaving to make sure that he or she understands what your gliders eat, how to prepare their meals, and how to keep their cage and dishes clean. Instruct your helper about proper methods of handling and let the gliders become familiar with their future sitter over several sessions so that they will not be scared of the person (or vice versa) when you leave.

All the instructions you give your helper regarding your pet's care should be written down and left near the glider's cage. It would also be a good idea to offer them this book to read and refer to. Leave a phone number where you can be reached in case the caretaker has any questions or concerns and check in occasionally to make sure that everything is going according to plan. Your veterinarian's phone number should also be included on the list in case there are any medical emergencies during your absence.

DIET

You will have to do a little experimenting and juggling of various combinations of foods in order to strike a happy balance between what your glider likes and what is nutritionally good for it.

A sugar glider's diet in captivity consists primarily of fresh fruits and vegetables as well as various sources of protein such as meats, egg, tofu, insects, rodents, and dairy products. Overall, the diet should contain about 24 percent protein.

Fruits and Vegetables

Sugar gliders enjoy a wide range of fruits and vegetables—of course, they tend to prefer sweet varieties. However, individual gliders have differing likes and dislikes. You may also find that your pet glider's preferences change over time.

Fruits and vegetables should be fed fresh every evening. Feed three or four types of fruits and vegetables in varying combinations

Food is not just for nutrition. It is a primary source of enjoyment and stimulation.

each night. In emergencies I have resorted to feeding canned fruit packed in *unsweetened* pear juice, but I don't make a habit of it because canned fruits are often deficient in nutrients compared to their fresh counterparts.

It is not necessary to cut fruit into tiny bite-size pieces. I often give my gliders apples, oranges, and cantaloupes that have only been quartered or cut into large chunks. The gliders eat the fruit flesh and leave the peel behind.

Some people prefer to put all the fruits and vegetables together in a blender and then pour the resulting slurry into ice cube trays. The frozen cubes make convenient small portions that can be left in a bowl to defrost in the cage before going to bed. However, if there is something in the mixture that your glider doesn't like, you may find that it rejects the whole concoction.

All fruits and vegetables should be thoroughly rinsed to remove pesticide residues.

Remove any uneaten food from the cage the following morning to avoid having it spoil and attract vermin. Wash and sanitize the feeding bowls in preparation for the next feeding.

Do *not* feed dry fruit and nut mixes. Some feed companies are guilty of selling these mixes as sugar glider food, but they are not suitable and certainly should not be fed as an exclusive diet. These mixes often contain preservatives and added salt and sugar. Nuts contain significant amounts of fat and phosphorus and, if allowed to, sugar gliders will eat them to excess and soon become malnourished. An overabundance of phosphorus in the diet can interfere with calcium absorption, leading to calcium deficiency and metabolic bone disease. Too much fat can lead to obesity and other health problems (see Health Concerns, page 77). In addition, sugar gliders do not find dried fruit nearly as palatable as fresh fruit because some

individuals do not actually swallow the fruit flesh but rather chew it until all the juice and flavor has been extracted and then spit out the pulp. This kind of behavior is especially apparent in wild caught gliders that are accustomed to feeding primarily on tree sap.

Sugar gliders do love sweet things, but they should not be fed raw sugar, sugar substitutes, or candy, and should never be given chocolate.

Red Meat, Poultry, Eggs, and Tofu

Meat and poultry should be lean, cooked (but not fried), and cut into very small pieces or minced. Do not feed leftover meats that have salt, sauces, or spices added to them. Processed meats often have added salt and preservatives and should be avoided. Chicken should be fed skinless and boneless. Chicken skin is undesirable because it is very high in fat. Poultry bones splinter easily to form sharp points and edges that could potentially inflict injuries to a sugar glider's mouth, throat, and digestive tract.

Eggs and boned meats are low in calcium and magnesium. They are also high in phosphorus, which compounds the relative lack of calcium. These items should not be used as the main source of protein in the diet unless supplemental calcium is provided to make up the deficit. Hard-boiled eggs can be fed chopped or mashed.

Tofu is a good source of protein and it has the advantage of containing higher amounts of calcium in relation to its phosphorus content (the same is true of yogurt). If you cannot get your glider to eat plain tofu, then try cutting it into very small pieces and mix it with a pureed fruit that it likes. You could also try adding a small amount of honey or yogurt to the mixture.

Live Treats

In the wild, sugar gliders get most of their protein from insects and small vertebrates. They love crickets, grasshoppers, moths, butterflies, mealworms, and earthworms (if you can stand to watch your glider eat them like licorice). Insects can often be purchased from pet stores. They can be fed frozen or live in a smooth sided dish that they cannot easily crawl out of.

Live insects really get a glider's attention. A sugar glider's whole demeanor changes when it catches sight of moving prey, and it is amazing how quickly it can pounce and dispatch its quarry. It really gives one an insight into how efficient wild gliders are as predators.

I do not recommend feeding more than one or two mealworms or crickets to a glider each evening. Mealworms are quite high in fat, and, like most insects, they lack adequate calcium in relation to their phosphorus content.

Do not collect insects outdoors where they may have been sprayed with pesticides or become parasitized.

Pinky Mice

A pinky mouse is a mouse pup that has not yet grown any fur. You can often pick up frozen pinky mice at your local pet store. Furred juvenile and adult rodents can also be fed as long as you don't mind removing the pelt in the morning. Juvenile or adult rodents are superior from a nutritional perspective because they have a calcified skeleton and thus are a better source of calcium than newborn pups, which do not develop a substantially mineralized skeleton until they are a week or so old. However, if the pinky mouse pups have recently nursed, they do have sufficient calcium within their system.

Do not defrost or microwave the frozen rodents prior to putting them in your glider's cage. I have found that my gliders will chew on them even though they are frozen and they will defrost gradually over the course of the night anyway. In this way, the remains, if there are any, will not be spoiled when you remove them from the cage in the morning. It is necessary to be extremely careful with raw meats and raw egg because there is always the remote possibility of contamination with *Salmonella* and other bacteria (see Health Concerns, page 77).

Dairy Products

Dairy products such as cottage cheese and naturally cultured yogurt are good nutritious sources of protein.

Lactose is a sugar or carbohydrate found in milk and noncultured dairy products. Most marsupials have very low levels of lactose in their milk and will suffer from lactose intolerance if they are fed lactose-rich milks such as cow's milk and goat's milk. This is especially true of macropods (wallabies and kangaroos). However, sugar gliders, and the possum family in general, are capable of successfully metabolizing more lactose than that contained within their own milk. The process by which they do this is complicated, but the end result is that they do not tend to suffer from gas, bloating, and diarrhea, which are the signs associated with lactose intolerance, after consuming dairy products. Nevertheless, it is always better to err on the side of caution. Cottage cheese is relatively low in lactose (compared with the raw milk from which it is made). Yogurt contains lactose in a more digestible form than that found in raw milk.

Dry Cat Food?

For years, many pet owners and breeders have satisfied their glider's protein requirements primarily with dry cat food. However, there is some concern among animal care specialists and nutritional experts that the long-term use of cat food, especially in excess, may impact negatively upon sugar glider health and potentially shorten their life span. Dry cat food is often artificially preserved and may exceed a sugar glider's requirements for protein, vitamin A, and vitamin D. The nutritionists that I consulted recommended substituting cooked meats and egg, insects, rodents, and tofu.

If you choose to use a dry cat food, do so in very small amounts as an occasional treat. Use a high quality brand and don't allow your gliders free choice access to it. I don't recommend feeding canned cat food at all because, in my experience, gliders will not eat it. They do however like to play in it, which makes an unpleasant, smelly mess.

Nuts

The only thing a sugar glider likes more than a nut is two nuts. Nuts are a good source of protein, but they are also high in fat and phosphorus. *Nuts and sunflower seeds should be strictly rationed.* Breeders and pet owners who have let their gliders eat nuts freely over a long period of time have invariably found that their gliders have suffered from poor health. A nut or two occasionally as a treat is more than enough.

All nuts should be raw, not roasted, and should be unsalted. Gliders particularly like peanuts, sunflower seeds, pecans, and unsweetened coconut. Nuts such as sunflower seeds and peanuts can be offered in the shell.

Water

Fresh water should be available to your glider at all times. A sugar glider's diet contains a lot of high-water-content items, and so you will find that it will not drink a great deal each night. It is still necessary to provide fresh water even when fruit juice is included with the evening meal.

Water bottles should be cleaned and sanitized daily. Water dishes need to be cleaned even more frequently because standing water can easily become contaminated with stools, urine, and discarded food.

Balancing the Diet

It is important that your glider consume a well-rounded diet. This can be difficult to accomplish at times, especially when a sugar glider develops a favorite to the point that it ignores everything else. Sugar gliders will "pig

out" on nuts if you let them and will soon become malnourished. Some may overeat fatty foods and become obese. It may be necessary to ration favorite items in order to encourage your pet to eat a healthy mixture of foods. Likewise, if your glider develops a mania for a certain type of fruit, try rationing it or only feed that fruit on alternate days to encourage it to eat a selection. Those of you with children may already be familiar with these methods of persuasion.

As well as providing your glider with nutritious food items, it is also important to combine them in such a way that the overall diet contains at least twice as much calcium as it does phosphorous. This can be rather difficult to accomplish naturally because most of the food items fed to gliders have higher amounts of phosphorous in relation to calcium. Consult the nutritional values table included in this book on page 55. It lists the nutritional content of the food products commonly fed to gliders and will assist you in feeding items in appropriate combinations.

How Much to Feed?

In general, a sugar glider eats about $1/4$ to $1/3$ of a cup of mixed fruits and vegetables and one tablespoon of protein based product(s) per night. If you notice that all the food is gone in the morning, gradually increase the amount until there is a little bit left and then cut back slightly. If you notice that your glider is becoming obese on this amount of food, then cut back some more. Fat rich foods should be fed in smaller portions to obese animals.

Taronga Zoo Diet

Apple .1 oz (3 g)

Dog kibble .05 oz (1.5 g)

Grapes/kiwi .1 oz (3 g)

Sweet potato .1 oz (3 g)

Pear .07 oz (2 g)

Insects when available

Leadbeater's mix (see below)

Banana/corn .1 oz (3 g)

Fly pupae 1 teaspoon

Hard boiled egg .35 oz (10 g)

Orange .14 oz (4 g)

Day old chick once a week

Rockmelon/Paw Paw (if not available, substitute Papaya)

Leadbeater's Mix Ingredients (see Preparation below)

Warm water 15.84 fl oz (450 ml)

3 shelled boiled eggs

Vitamin and mineral supplements

Honey 15.84 fl oz (450 ml)

High protein baby cereal 2.64 oz (75 g)

Printed with permission from Taronga Zoo.

I have noticed that my gliders go through inexplicable cycles where for a period of weeks they will consistently eat the same amount of food in a night, and then, despite the fact that no changes have been made in the diet, they will eat very little for a period of two or three nights. Gliders in different buildings, with no contact whatsoever, will all decide to eat very little on the same nights. Perhaps they sense a change in the weather or atmospheric pressure. A few breeders I've talked to have commented on this phenomenon.

Alternative Diets

The diet listed above is used by the Taronga Zoo in Sydney, Australia, to feed their squirrel gliders. Squirrel gliders are slightly larger than sugar gliders and so it is likely that the amounts listed would provide for more than one feeding portion. One of the diet favorites is the Leadbeater's mix.

To prepare the Leadbeater's Mix: After removing the shells from the hard boiled eggs, blend them until they are a paste. Mix the water and honey together in a separate bowl until the honey dissolves. Add half of the honey and water mix to the blended eggs and blend. Add the remainder of the honey and water and repeat blending. Add the vitamins and minerals along with half the baby cereal and blend. Add the remaining baby cereal and blend. Continue to blend until mixture is lump free.

Psittacine Diet

At least one North American zoo uses pelleted psittacine (parrot) food as the core of its sugar gliders' diet. By providing a nutritionally balanced, prepared feed such as the psittacine pellets, the amount of fresh produce in the diet can be reduced, the type of high moisture content feeds offered becomes less critical, and the necessity for supplementation is reduced. The sample diet appears below. The amounts listed are suitable for one sugar glider.

Do not confuse pelleted psittacine diet with parrot mix (a dry fruit and nut mixture). They are two entirely different things. The brand of psittacine diet used in the example below is often available in pet stores under the brand name "Scenic Birdfood."

I do feed psittacine diet occasionally in small amounts, but it does not constitute the bulk of my gliders' diet. The diets that zoos feed must not only be nutritionally efficient but they must also be expedient to prepare and deliver. Because I only have a small number of animals (compared to a zoo), I can afford to spend more time preparing fresh foods for my gliders and I prefer to do this. My philosophy is that a captive animal's food is not merely a source of nutrition. It is also one of its primary sources of enjoyment and stimulation. Therefore, every effort should be made not only to make the diet nutritious and well balanced, but also to make it pleasing in taste, texture, and variety.

Dietary Supplements

Pets that are fed foods in nutritionally balanced combinations and amounts should not require dietary supplements. However, sugar gliders can be finicky eaters. They can sometimes make it extremely difficult to balance their diet simply by refusing to eat anything but their favorite food items. If, despite your best efforts, you suspect that your glider's nutritional intake is lacking, you may have to resort to feeding supplements. Supplementation may also be necessary to improve or maintain the health of sick, elderly, and nursing gliders.

It is always best to consult your veterinarian before adding vitamins and minerals to your pet's food. It is also important to follow the directions carefully to avoid the possibility of overdosing your pet. More is *not* necessarily better.

Multivitamins and Minerals

The following is a list of some of the brands of vitamins and minerals commonly used by zoos, pet owners, and breeders:

Nekton-Lori: This multivitamin and protein supplement was originally developed for birds. It is a powder designed to be mixed with water

Psittacine Diet

Psittacine diet, jungle, mixed flavor	15 pieces	5.3 g
Banana, peeled		2.5 g
Grape, halved	1	3.0 g
Honeydew	½ inch (1.25 cm) cube	5.0 g
Papaya	½ inch (1.25 cm) cube	3.5 g
*Crickets, adult	3	1.0 g
*Mealworm larvae	5	4.0 g

*Insect prey are maintained on a high calcium cricket diet prior to feeding and thus have a higher calcium content than the insects purchased in pet stores.

to make a nectar. However, many glider keepers sprinkle an eighth of a teaspoonful (a pinch between finger and thumb) over a favorite piece of fruit or add it to apple juice instead. This supplement contains calcium and phosphorus in a 1:1 ratio, so it cannot be relied upon as a calcium supplement. If it is made into a nectar, it spoils quickly and should not be left out in a bowl for more than a few hours.

Gliderade: Gliderade seems somewhat similar to Nekton-Lori in that it is designed to be fed as a nectar substitute. It is lower in protein than Nekton-Lori, but it is also a lot cheaper to buy.

Vionate: This multivitamin is in powdered form and has calcium and phosphorus in a more desirable ratio of 2:1. If you go by the dosage for hamsters and small birds, they recommend one eighth of a teaspoon per day, per animal. It is best sprinkled over a favorite piece of fruit.

Reptivite: This multivitamin is an ultra fine powder that contains the full spectrum of vitamins, minerals (calcium and phosphorus in a 2:1 ratio), electrolytes, and amino acids. The directions recommend that a very small amount be dusted over fruits or vegetables or that insects be placed in a plastic bag along with the supplement and shaken until the insects are lightly coated.

Calcium Supplements: My veterinarian recommended that I use a calcium supplement that did not use a calcium phosphate as its source of calcium because the gliders get plenty of phosphorus in their diet. He also recommended supplementing vitamin D_3 along with the calcium as this aids in calcium absorption.

There are many calcium supplements on the market. It is best to choose a phosphorus free one that is in powdered form and already has D_3 added to it.

Rep-Cal: This supplement is described as phosphorus-free calcium with vitamin D_3 in an ultra fine powder. The recommended dosage is $1/2$ tablespoon per pound (450 g) of food. The directions specify that it be sprinkled over fruits and vegetables or dusted over insects. The same company also makes a multivitamin similar to Reptivite called Rep-Cal Herptivite. They recommend using the Herptivite and the calcium in combination. The two are not sold premixed because the ingredients are not compatible from a storage perspective.

Specialty Products

As the popularity of sugar gliders has increased, numerous companies have sprung up to capitalize on the demand for glider products. Many offer a wide range of items including food, cages, and toys. While some of these products might be very good, keep in mind that something packaged and described as suitable for sugar gliders may not necessarily be ideal for its specified purpose. Read the labels carefully and critically. In the case of a food item, look at the listed ingredients. Remember, the ingredients should be in the order of most to least. If the first ingredient is sugar, then obviously it could be more accurately described as "candy" than "food." Ask yourself who formulated the product. Was an animal nutritionist involved in its development? I personally believe that fresh foods are better than processed.

Nutritional Content of Common Sugar Glider Foods

Food Item (not suggested serving size)	Calories gms	Protein gms	Carbohydrates gms	Total fat mg	Calcium mg	Phosphorus
Apple, raw, cored, peeled, ½ cup	32	0.1	8.4	0.2	2	4
Avocado, peeled, pitted, ½ cup	185	12.3	8.5	17.6	13	49
Banana, peeled, ½ cup	104	1.2	26.4	0.5	7	22
Beef, ground, extra lean, cooked, 4 oz.	298	31.7	0	18.1	40	736
Cantaloupe, trimmed, cubed, ½ cup	29	0.7	6.7	0.2	9	14
Carrot, raw, ½ cup	24	0.6	5.6	0.1	15	24
Cottage cheese, low fat, ½ cup	101	15.5	4.1	2.2	77	170
Cherry, pitted, ½ cup	39	0.8	9.4	0.2	12	12
Chicken, meat only, cooked, 4 oz.	171	32.9	0	3.4	17	221
Coconut, raw, shelled, 1.6 oz.	159	1.5	6.9	15.1	6	51
Corn, sweet, fresh, raw, 3.2 oz. ear	77	2.9	17.1	1.1	2	80
Egg, hard boiled in shell, 1 large	77	6.3	0.6	5.3	25	86
Fig, dried, uncooked, ½ cup	254	3	65	1.2	143	68
Grape, American, peeled, seedless, ½ cup	29	0.3	7.9	0.2	7	5
Grapefruit, pink, sections, ½ cup	43	0.6	11.1	0.1	13	10
Honeydew, cubed, ½ cup	30	0.4	7.8	0.1	5	9
Kiwifruit, 1 medium, approx. 3.1 oz.	46	0.8	11.3	0.3	20	31
Mango, peeled, seeded, ½ cup	54	0.4	14	0.2	9	9
Orange, trimmed sections, ½ cup	13	0.3	3.3	<.1	33	16
Papaya, peeled, seeded, ½ cup	27	0.4	6.9	0.1	17	4
Peach, peeled, pitted, ½ cup	37	0.6	9.4	0.1	5	11
Peanut, raw, 1 oz.	159	7.2	4.5	13.8	26	105
Pear, with skin, ½ cup	49	0.3	12.5	0.3	10	9
Peas, green, sweet, raw, shelled, ½ cup	58	3.9	10.4	0.3	18	77
Pineapple, diced, ½ cup	39	0.3	9.6	0.3	6	6
Plum, pitted, ½ cup	46	0.7	10.7	0.5	3	4
Prune, dried, pitted, 4 oz.	271	3	71.1	0.6	58	90
Raisin, seedless, 1 oz.	85	0.9	22.4	0.1	14	27
Raspberry, fresh, trimmed, ½ cup	31	0.6	7.7	0.3	14	8
Strawberry, fresh, trimmed, ½ cup	23	0.15	5.2	0.3	11	14
Sunflower seed, shelled, raw, dried, 1 oz.	162	6.5	5.3	14.1	8	50
Sweet potato, raw, 1 medium, approx. 6.3 oz.	136	2.1	31.6	0.4	29	37
Tofu, raw, firm, ½ cup	183	19.9	5.4	11	258	239
Yogurt, plain, low fat, 8 oz.	144	11.9	16	3.5	415	326

Source: Adapted from *The Encyclopedia of Food Values*, Corinne T. Netzer. New York: Dell Publishing, 1992.

REPRODUCTIVE BIOLOGY

Sugar gliders will breed year-round in captivity. Adult females have an estrous cycle of 29 days.

External Sex Characteristics

Like the majority of marsupials, female sugar gliders have a pouch on their abdomens in roughly the spot one would expect to see the navel on a placental mammal. Male gliders have a furred scrotum about the size of a pea on their lower abdomen.

Scent Glands

A mature male glider can be differentiated from a female, at a glance, by a distinctive diamond shaped bald spot on the top of his head. This bald spot is a scent gland that is absent in females and not apparent in immature males. Males have another scent gland on their chest. Both males and females have scent glands in their perineal area.

The Cloacal Aperture

The cloaca or "common sewer" is an anatomical feature typical of marsupials. The reproductive system, urinary ducts, and alimentary tract all open into the cloaca so that only one orifice is apparent at the base of the tail. In contrast, placental mammals have separate external urinogenital and anal openings.

The male's penis can sometimes be seen protruding from the cloacal aperture when he is cleaning himself. Some veterinarians have gotten a chuckle out of clients who have run into their clinics in a panic because they think their sugar glider has a large pink worm protruding from its bottom and is in dire need of deworming. Other people have mistaken their pet's penis for severe hemorrhoids or a prolapsed rectum.

By being familiar with your pet's anatomy, you can avoid being a source of amusement to your veterinarian and save yourself some anxiety.

Internal Reproductive Anatomy

In the female glider, eggs are shed into separate horns of a divided uterus to be fertilized. There are also two separate vaginae and cer-

Female   **Male**

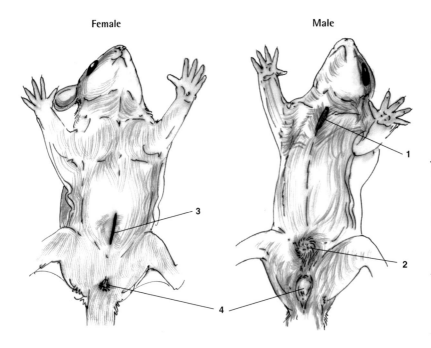

1. *The chest gland is only apparent on mature males.*
2. *The scrotum on a baby male looks like a wart on its lower abdomen. Adult males have furred scrotums.*
3. *The pouch opening.*
4. *The cloacal aperture. The male's penis can sometimes be seen protruding from this orifice.*

vices. In most marsupials, the babies are delivered through a central birth canal which forms before each birth, although in the kangaroo family, this canal, once formed, is permanent.

The female's "double" reproductive organs are matched by the male's penis, which is bifurcated (divided in two).

Reproduction and Development

Mating

Sugar glider pairs mate frequently and are not secretive about it. They will persist in their activities even after they realize that they are being observed.

Sexing gliders that are not tame may require gloves.

During mating the male grasps the fur on the female's back in his forefeet to hold her in place. I have never seen a male use his teeth to restrain the female. In this respect they are much gentler than many of the opossum family.

Pregnancy and Birth

Sugar gliders are born weighing only 0.007 ounce (0.19 gram) and measuring barely 0.2 inch (5 millimeters) in length, after a gestation of only 16 days. Once born, the tiny pink infant embarks on a journey up its mother's abdomen to the pouch opening. Its eyelids are fused shut and the eye within is still in the process of developing. The ears too, are fused, and appear as mere nubs on either side of the head. Since the baby is both blind and deaf, it makes the five-minute journey to the pouch by instinct alone and completely unaided by its mother. If the baby loses its grip and falls to the ground or fails to find the pouch opening, it cannot be retrieved by its mother and will quickly die. The

joey's safe arrival in the pouch is truly one of nature's miracles.

If you happen to see your glider give birth and

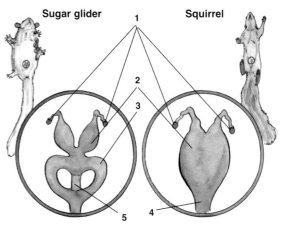

Marsupial v. placental reproductive tracts:
1. Ovaries, 2. Uterus, 3. Lateral vagina,
4. Vagina, 5. Central birth canal

you notice the baby losing its grip and falling off, you might be able to intervene by picking the baby up and gently placing it at the pouch opening. In order to do this, you will need at least one assistant. While one person holds the female glider so that she is lying on her back with her abdomen uppermost, the second person must place the baby glider on the female's stomach, immediately adjacent to the pouch opening. Once the baby has been placed next to the pouch, the second person must attend the baby closely to make sure that it doesn't fall off again. If the baby glider can't find its own way into the pouch, it may be possible to lift the edge of the pouch opening slightly and try to gently guide the baby inside. This technique has been used successfully with larger marsupials. However, I only know of one such endeavor to save a newborn sugar glider. Unfortunately, the attempt was not successful because the baby sustained some damage from its fall.

Life in the Pouch

Once within the safety of its mother's warm, humid pouch, the joey seeks out one of the four nipples contained within and takes it into its mouth. Gliders at this stage of development do not have the jaw muscles necessary for sucking milk. Instead, the nipple swells, making it difficult for the joey to disconnect, and milk is expressed into its mouth automatically. The joey remains engaged with the nipple until its jaw is developed enough that it is able to disconnect and suck milk at will.

As the joey develops, its presence becomes more obvious as it increases in size and distends the pouch. At the two month stage, the pouch looks as if it has one or two extremely large peanuts stuffed in it. The arms, legs, and tail may protrude from the pouch opening when the youngster moves around, and soon thereafter the joey begins to emerge from the pouch.

Post-Pouch Development

A sugar glider emerges from the pouch with great reluctance once it becomes too cramped for it to remain any longer. The body emerges tail first but the joey may persist in keeping its head inside the pouch for several more days before that too is allowed to come out for the first time. At this stage, the glider is approximately two months old and is fully furred (although the fur is shorter than it will be later on). The eyes are often closed initially but open within a week to ten days of emergence. From this point on, the joey will put its head back in the pouch only to feed and will ride on the back or stomach of one of its parents.

Adult male sugar gliders are not exempt from baby-sitting and can frequently be seen carrying their offspring. The males

The baby joey suckles milk within its mother's warm and humid pouch.

seem very attentive and caring in their attitudes toward their young.

Independence and Sexual Maturity

Five-month-old sugar gliders are fully independent and are capable of finding and catching their own food in the wild. At eight months old, some of them have already reached sexual maturity, but on average most become sexually mature at 12 to 14 months of age.

RAISING YOUR OWN GLIDERS

Watching gliders grow from lumps in the pouch to friendly and inquisitive pets is fascinating. However, the decision to breed an animal is something that should be well thought out and planned for.

Breeding gliders is rewarding from a number of perspectives. While you may not see the babies being born or making the journey to the pouch, you will be able to watch in wonder as the babies grow, distend the pouch, reluctantly emerge, and open their eyes. You will be able to witness firsthand, the heartwarming way the mother and father cooperate to care for their young.

The production of baby sugar gliders should not be a mere side effect of having adult male and female gliders in the same cage. Before you embark on a breeding program consider these questions:

• Are your animals suitable as breeding stock? If they are related they should not be allowed to breed.

The production of healthy baby sugar gliders can be a fun and rewarding experience.

• Are you willing and able to comply with the USDA's licensing standards for breeding? Can you afford the license?
• Do you have enough time to handle the babies regularly in order to make them tame?
• Do you have the time to hand-rear babies that have been orphaned or rejected? Can you afford the costly milk formula and the veterinary bills associated with such infants?
• Will you be able to find suitable homes for the babies once they are weaned?
• Have you budgeted for the cost of advertising the babies?
• Can you cope with the heartache and anxiety involved with parting with an animal that you have invested time, money, and love in?
• If you keep the resulting offspring, it will be necessary to provide separate cages or to neuter animals to prevent inbreeding. Are your existing cages big enough to house your pets and their adult offspring? Do you have the

space and money for extra cages? Can you afford the veterinary bills associated with neutering a glider?

A License to Breed

It is not necessary in most states to have a license to keep sugar gliders as pets, but it may be necessary to have a United States Department of Agriculture license in order to breed, sell, and broker gliders. Check with the appropriate USDA sector office regarding licensing requirements (see Useful Addresses, page 91).

It is not difficult or expensive to obtain a license. The USDA is concerned that animals are adequately housed and cared for and may want to inspect your premises prior to issuing a license and periodically thereafter.

Choosing Breeding Stock

There are three categories of sugar glider available on the market: Hand-tame, domestically raised, and wild-caught gliders.

Hand-tame animals are usually purchased as babies. The advantage of buying tame stock— apart from the obvious one that they are also excellent pets—is that you know for sure that you are buying young animals that are not someone else's castoffs that are elderly or barren. The only disadvantage to buying hand-tame babies as breeding stock is that it will be several months before they are old enough to breed.

Sugar gliders advertised as domestically raised are not necessarily tame and they might not be babies. However, they have been captive-bred. You can sometimes tell the difference between domestically raised and wild-caught adults from Indonesia by the color. Recently

imported animals tend to be a brownish orange rather than the steely silver gray of captive-bred animals. There are many theories as to what causes this color variation. Some people believe the brown coloration is due to genetic factors, but if this were true, the brown gliders' captive-born babies would be brown too and this is not the case. It is more likely that the brown coloration of the fur is due to staining, either from environmental factors such as staining from tree sap or perhaps scent gland staining due to being closely confined prior to and during shipping. Some breeders believe that by feeding a certain diet or supplement, they have caused the brown gliders' fur to turn gray, but I think it's more likely that the animals simply shed their fur slowly over a long period of time, and the new fur is gray because it is not being restained. I have seen gliders that have been in the country for about eight months that are mottled with patches of brown and patches of gray. Eventually these animals become completely gray.

Wild-caught gliders are usually considerably cheaper than hand-tame and domestically bred gliders, but there are disadvantages: Wild-caught gliders are often parasitized and are more prone to shipping stress and stress-related illness and death. However, once they have been in captivity for a year or so, they are indistinguishable from nontame, domestically bred animals. Imported animals take longer to settle in and start to breed, but once they get started, they breed just as readily as domestic stock. There is also the disadvantage of not knowing how old your gliders are. They might be young or they might be geriatric.

Even imported animals gradually come around to the point where they will not run

away when you enter the aviary, and some individuals may even take fruit from your hand or hop down onto your shoulder. However, it is unlikely that you will ever be able to close a hand around an imported or nontame adult without causing it to panic and eventually bite if it is not released.

If you decide to buy wild-caught stock, try to get some that have been in the country for at least a few months.

Sugar Gliders of a Different Color

Sugar gliders have been extensively bred in captivity for several decades. It's not surprising that anomalies in color have started to crop up. The most striking examples are the albino gliders. An albino is an animal that is lacking in pigmentation. It usually has red eyes and white fur. While albinos do occur naturally in wild

populations, they are extremely uncommon. These animals rarely live to maturity, and therefore don't usually survive to pass along their genes. Sugar gliders are nocturnal, and their primary predators in the wild are birds of prey. It wouldn't take an owl very long to notice a bright white sugar glider at night.

Albino gliders are still very scarce in captivity and demand high prices when they are offered for sale. It is possible for two outwardly normal gliders to produce an albino baby if they are both carriers of the recessive gene. Also of note are white gliders with dark eyes and gliders with white-tipped tails. These are not different species but rather color variations and mutations within the species.

There are also subtle variations in color that are harder to categorize. Some animals appear a lighter gray or brown than average, and some breeders put a price differential on such animals describing them as "platinum" or "beige"

gliders, but often they don't breed true and it isn't unusual for them to change color as they get older.

Colony Breeding vs. Breeding in Pairs and Trios

There are two ways of breeding sugar gliders. They can be bred in colonies of up to 12 animals in a communal aviary or they can be divided into pairs and trios. There are advantages and disadvantages to both approaches.

Colony breeding is nice from the perspective that it is a more natural situation because gliders tend to form groups in the wild. A group of gliders in a large aviary is more interesting to watch, and they have more room to leap around than animals that are split up into pairs and trios and that are probably consigned to smaller cages. You can feed, water, and clean a cage containing 12 gliders in one-sixth the time it takes to feed, water, and clean six cages containing two gliders. However, gliders in large groups do not reproduce as successfully as

gliders in pairs and trios. There is a much higher incidence of pouch babies disappearing in larger groups. One can only assume they have been eaten.

Even though one male is capable of impregnating up to ten females, the chances of your finding a breeder who is willing to sell you one male and ten females is remote. In an aviary situation it is more likely that there will be a mixture of males and females. Because one male tends to become dominant and do most if not all of the breeding, the rest of the males are redundant from a breeding perspective. When you go to sell the babies, you will not be able to sell unrelated pairs (unless you have more than one colony) because it is likely that the offspring from different mothers all have the same father.

The advantage of pair and trio breeding, apart from those already stated of higher production, better utilization of males for breeding, and more genetic variation in the offspring, is that it is much easier to keep track of individuals with respect to how much they are eating, what their nutritional preferences are, and how well they are reproducing.

Record Keeping

If you have a large number of animals you will need to keep written records in order to keep track of health, fertility, litter size, parenting ability, temperament, and so on. This will help you to identify those animals that are good breeders and those animals that should be culled from the breeding program.

Housing Colonies

The bigger the group, the larger the cage should be. I have aviaries that house anywhere from eight to 12 gliders of mixed gender and that range in size from 4 × 4 × 7 feet high (1.2 × 1.2 × 2.1 m) to 4 × 8 × 7 feet high (1.2 × 2.4 × 2.1 m).

My husband built some of my bigger aviary frames out of slotted metal angle (that was originally designed for building industrial shelving) and the wire was then bolted to the frames. The aviary ceilings are wood and covered in half inch chicken wire so that the gliders can scamper across the ceiling if they want to. We attached wheels to the wooden floor to make the large cages easier to move for cleaning purposes. The entry doors are as small as practically possible in order to minimize the possibility of escape. However, I haven't found that the gliders try to get out when I go in.

Feeding Colonies

Obviously, it is necessary to increase the amount of food being fed in proportion to the number of gliders in the cage. It is also prudent to provide several feeding and watering sites. If only one such site is provided, you might find that there is an excessive amount of fighting at meal times with the more dominant animals making off with the lion's share of the choice morsels.

Nesting Boxes for Colonies

Keep in mind that nesting boxes for colonies need to be bigger than those provided for pairs and trios. Providing several small nesting boxes

keep clean, and the gliders show no interest in chewing them.

Replacing Lost Mates and Introducing New Animals

If you are unfortunate and lose the male or female from a paired couple, the remaining glider will except a new mate, but you must be cautious when introducing the new animal.

Quarantine any new animal that you purchase for at least three weeks before you introduce it to your resident stock. Watch the new animal carefully during the quarantine period to make sure that it is healthy and eating well. You don't want to expose your stock to a potentially sick animal.

The process of introduction is the same whether you are introducing a new male or a new female. When you introduce the new animal to the cage housing your other gliders, stay and watch to make sure that there is not an excessive amount of fighting. You should expect some small skirmishes and some disgruntled noises, but there should not be any bloodshed. Introduce the animal during the day, and hopefully within a few minutes it will be curled up with the others in the nesting box. By the time they all wake up in the evening, the stranger should smell enough like the group that it will be readily accepted as one of the gang.

If you notice that the newly introduced animal persists in sleeping on its own, typically curled up in a food dish or even down on the floor, or shows signs of having been badly bitten, remove the glider from that situation because it has probably been rejected by the group and they may eventually kill it.

instead of one big one will not work because gliders like to sleep together in a big huddle. A medium size polypropylene or polyethylene plastic storage container works well as a nesting box for larger groups. Make a hole in one side or end with a doorknob hole saw and drill some ventilation holes around the side and in the lid. The lid can be easily removed for access, the plastic containers are durable and easy to

Provide the rejected glider with a cage of its own and place it next to the enclosure containing the rest of your gliders. Every evening, switch the nesting boxes around so that the rejected animal sleeps in the other glider's nesting box and vice versa. In this way, the gliders can get acquainted with each other's scents without having any physical contact with one another. After a week, try reintroducing the new animal. You might have to repeat this procedure several times before you are successful.

It is not a good idea to try and introduce a recent weanling to a cage containing adult gliders because the weanling may try and ride on the backs of the adults as if they were its parents. The adult gliders will be irritated by a strange weanling trying to cling to them and may respond aggressively. Wait until the weanling is at least $3/4$ adult size before you try and introduce it to a cage containing adults.

Pets as Breeding Stock

Many pet owners are concerned that their pet glider may not stay tame if they breed it, but they need not be concerned. In my experience, a sugar glider's personality does not change as a result of being bred. It is not necessary to stop handling them or to give them additional privacy in order to get them to breed, and you can continue handling your female pet even after you notice that she has bulges in her pouch.

When to Breed

While it is true that some species of animals will breed prematurely if allowed to, this is not true of sugar gliders. Males and females do not need to be kept in separate cages until they reach sexual maturity because they will only breed when they are fully mature at eight to 14 months of age or older.

Separation of Expectant Females

If your expectant female is in a colony situation, then you may want to put her in a separate cage, with just one other glider for company, as an added precaution until she has weaned her babies. This should not be necessary if the female is caged with just one or two other animals. Males do not act aggressively toward their offspring and may even be seen carrying them around on their backs after they emerge from the pouch.

Dietary Requirements for Breeding

Pregnancy and lactation make additional demands on the mother's physical resources, so special care must be taken to ensure that she is eating a healthy diet. You might notice that your female glider eats slightly more when she has babies in her pouch and she may eat her protein based foods such as pinky mice, insects, egg, and tofu, with more relish than she did previously. It may be necessary to provide supplemental calcium to compensate for the demands of pregnancy and nursing.

Frequency of Breeding and Its Effect on Health

Gliders kept in pairs and trios will produce two or three litters a year. Gliders kept in a communal aviary are somewhat less prolific. If you do not separate the babies from the parents at weaning, this will sometimes cause a delay in breeding and you will achieve a lower annual production.

If allowed to, some sugar gliders will produce one litter of babies straight after another without any breaks in between. Some females will lose condition under these circumstances. If you have a female that has produced two to three litters, one right after the other, remove the male from the cage to prevent rebreeding for a couple of months and to give her an opportunity to rest and recover.

Litter Size and Gender Ratios

Sometimes there is just one baby in a litter, but two is more usual. A sugar glider female has four nipples in her pouch; so, theoretically, four babies are a possibility, but the largest litter I have heard of is three. It was once believed that sugar gliders always produced twins of the same sex. However, this is not true. You might have a litter of two males, two females, or a male and a female.

Detection of Babies in the Pouch

It is very unusual to see a sugar glider give birth or to see the babies making the climb to the pouch. In four years, I have been lucky enough to see this miracle take place once. I noticed that my pet female, Polly, seemed unusually interested in her pouch and was cleaning it repetitively. She did this while sitting out in the open, on a shelf in her cage, at a busy pet fair. I assumed that she already had a small baby in her pouch and was grooming it, as marsupial mothers are wont to do. Then I saw something very small and pink climbing up her abdomen toward her pouch. I couldn't believe that she could be so nonchalant about the whole thing. While the baby climbed, Polly groomed herself to remove the birthing fluids but she did not assist the baby in any way. Undaunted, the tiny creature hoisted itself upward and deftly tucked itself inside her pouch. Polly went back about her business as if nothing had happened and indeed, to look at her still flat pouch, one would think that nothing had.

If a baby has only just moved up into the pouch, its presence is not immediately apparent because it is so small. Some staining around the pouch area or an increase in the female's interest in her pouch are the only indications that she might have a new baby. It takes about two weeks for the joey to get large enough to be detectable as a very slight bulge that is still easy to miss. Within a month, the female will look as if she has one or two peanut size lumps

Within a month, the babies look like peanut-sized lumps inside the pouch. If there is just one baby, the pouch will appear lopsided.

inside her pouch. If she has two joeys, you will see a bulge on either side of the pouch opening. If she has a single joey, the pouch will appear lopsided.

As the babies get bigger, the pouch becomes increasingly distended and you may see arms and legs protrude from the pouch opening. The best way to get a look at your female's underside and pouch area is to observe her when she is clinging to the wire of the cage.

Don't try to manipulate the pouch to look inside at the babies. It is a delicate structure and youngsters can become prematurely dislodged from the nipples. *Never* try and pull a joey out of the pouch, even if it looks ready to come out. Let it come out in its own good time.

Handling the Babies

About a month after you notice peanut size bulges, the baby glider will emerge, and a week to ten days later the eyes will open. Once the glider's eyes have opened, you can start to handle it for short periods of time once or twice a day. It is easier to handle the baby during the day, rather than in the evening, because it can be taken from the nesting box while its parents are sleeping. In general, sugar gliders do not put up much of a fuss about having their babies handled. If you have an unusually possessive mother or father who acts aggressively when you try to touch its offspring, put on a pair of clean leather gloves to reach in and take the baby. Remove the gloves once you have the

Baby gliders enjoy being held and being kept warm. When they are little they are not too discriminating as to whether it's their mother holding them or a person. They have no fear of humans at this stage. Offer them a grape cut in half. You will find that they will only lick it at first, but as they get older they will start to bite at the grape flesh. By offering them food when you handle them, they will start to associate you with pleasant things and it will be easier to get them to eat when you take them away for weaning. If you leave the babies until they have been out of the pouch for several weeks before you start to handle them, you might find that you have to work harder with some individuals to gain their trust.

The offspring of wild-caught gliders are no more difficult to socialize and tame than those of hand-tame parents. However, it is very important to remove the offspring of wild-caught gliders for weaning at the earliest opportunity before they start to emulate their parents' wild behavior.

Weaning Babies

When a baby glider's eyes have been open for three weeks to a month, it is ready to be weaned. At first, the weanling may be a little upset at having been removed from his parents and the cage it was accustomed to. You may have to encourage the weanling by holding it and by offering it fruit. To guard against dehydration, encourage it to drink a small dish of apple juice. Put some pieces of fruit inside its nesting box, too. Make the fruit easier for it to handle by halving grapes and cutting fruit into small pieces. Pureed baby foods containing fruit, egg, and chicken can also be used.

baby in your hand because you want it to get used to your scent.

Wash your hands with an unscented soap prior to handling the baby to avoid getting anything on it that might be irritating to its parents.

Sometimes the baby might cling to one of its parents when you try to lift it away. Wrap your fingers around the baby and apply *gentle* traction to get it off. It will come off fairly easily. Do not pull on the joey's tail to try and get it to let go.

Weaning a glider at this stage should not be difficult. By the time a glider's eyes have been open for three weeks to a month, it has usually started to sample food from its parent's dish without any encouragement.

Some breeders recommend taking the babies away from the parents prematurely, as soon as the eyes open, and syringe feeding them. They feel that this makes the babies better pets. However, I have found this to be unnecessarily time-consuming, and it may deprive the youngster of the important early nutrition that it can best get from its mother. I have not noticed that it makes them any tamer.

Sexing Weanlings

Sexing babies and juveniles is only more difficult than sexing adults in the respect that baby males have not yet developed the distinctive bald spot on their foreheads that they will have once mature. The scrotum and the pouch area are just as easy to see on a baby as they are on an adult. A baby male that has only recently emerged from the pouch will not yet have grown any fur on his scrotum but it is still quite visible—it looks like a small heart-shaped wart on his lower abdomen. Likewise, a recently emerged female joey's pouch is very easy to see because the abdomen is the last part of the baby to grow fur.

Selling Weanlings

Once the baby gliders are eating well on their own, without any encouragement, they are ready to go to their new homes. It is best not to delay their sale (if you can bear to part with them) because the younger they are, the more easily they will bond with their new owner. Because sugar gliders are not overly prolific, most glider breeders find that they have a waiting list for their babies. It is just as important to be responsible when selling gliders as it is when buying them. Make sure the people that you sell your baby gliders to are knowledgeable about their care requirements. Encourage them to call if they have any questions or concerns once they get their baby home.

Avoiding Inbreeding

If it is not your intention to sell the offspring of your breeding stock, they should be separated from their parents and from siblings of the opposite sex, before they reach sexual maturity, in order to avoid inbreeding.

Breeders sometimes resort to line breeding in order to bring out a specific trait or recessive gene that is hard to isolate in any other way. In general, however, inbreeding should be avoided because inbred animals are often less vigorous and sometimes have physical deformities and mental deficits.

Neutering

If you decide that you no longer want to breed but you want to keep all your gliders together in the same cage, or you would like to keep a male baby but you do not want to risk inbreeding, it is possible to get your male gliders neutered by a veterinarian. Sugar gliders respond very well to volatile gaseous anesthetics and have been successfully neutered without any apparent ill effects.

Sugar gliders do not reject their babies very often. In general, they are excellent parents. If a glider does reject her baby, it is often because she is under stress. Stress can come from a variety of sources, but most often the culprit is poor health as a result of poor nutrition. Females that do not eat an adequate diet cannot produce enough milk for their joeys.

A rejected baby will often have bite marks on its body and will cry consistently because it is hungry. Quite often the baby is lethargic and cool to the touch. Always warm the baby up before you attempt to feed it because an animal suffering from hypothermia cannot swallow or digest its food efficiently.

Place the baby on a towel in a small glass or plastic aquarium and put the aquarium on top of a flat heating pad set on *low*. Check the bottom of the aquarium every few minutes for the first little while to make sure that it is not getting too hot. If the baby appears excessively cold, lethargic, and dehydrated, consult your veterinarian immediately. The baby's chances of survival might be improved by the subcutaneous administration of warmed fluids.

Once the joey has warmed up, offer it warm (not hot) puppy Esbilac in a dental syringe or a 1cc syringe. Mix one scoop of Esbilac powder to three scoops of water. Initially, you can add Pedialyte (available in most drug stores) to the formula instead of water to expedite rehydration. Puppy Esbilac and syringes can be purchased from most veterinarian's offices. Do not substitute Kitten Esbilac, goat's milk, cow's milk, or human milk replacer because they are all higher in lactose than puppy Esbilac and may cause colic and diarrhea.

There are milk formulas available that are designed specifically for marsupials. (See Information section for Biolac supplier.) The milk comes in several formulations depending on the level of development of the joey.

It is a good idea to acquire all the items that you will need to hand-rear a baby prior to needing them.

Offer the warmed formula one small drop at a time by placing it on the baby's lips. Do not try and force formula into the baby's mouth or try and feed it while it is crying; the baby may inadvertently inhale the formula into its lungs and develop aspiration pneumonia, which has a high mortality rate in very young animals. Feed the infant every two hours if it is not fully furred. If it is fully furred, feed every three to four

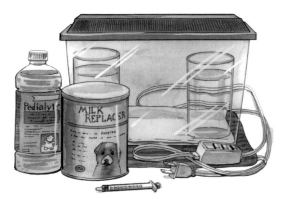

It is a good idea to gather all the supplies you will need to hand-rear a baby glider before an emergency arises.

REJECTED JOEY

hours. Once the glider's eyes are open, it is no longer necessary to feed during the night.

A baby glider has a very short attention span. It will often drink a few drops of formula and then lose interest. This does not necessarily mean that it is full. Put the baby down for a few seconds and then try feeding it again. You might find that its interest is renewed. Eventually, the baby will feel full and will stop feeding. The milk in the joey's stomach can be seen through the skin, as a lighter area in the glider's left abdomen.

If the baby develops diarrhea, feed it straight Pedialyte every other feeding until the diarrhea dries up. Don't confuse diarrhea with merely soft stools. Soft stools are acceptable, but they should not be liquid. Keep in mind that gliders urinate and defecate from the same orifice and so the stool may be accompanied by some urine. If the diarrhea is still present after 24 hours, consult your veterinarian. If there is blood in the stool, consult your veterinarian immediately.

At least twice a day, stimulate the baby to urinate and defecate by gently stroking the area between the base of the tail and the cloaca with a moistened cotton ball or swab. It is no longer necessary to do this once the baby's eyes have been open for about a week.

Hand-rearing joeys is not difficult, just time-consuming. Most do very well. However, joeys that are rejected or orphaned at a stage where they are still pink and semitransparent usually do not survive, despite the best efforts of the surrogate parent. It is important to keep these babies in a warm and humidified aquarium to try and more closely simulate the conditions found within the pouch. One can achieve this by placing two tall glasses of warm water in opposite corners of the aquarium and partially covering

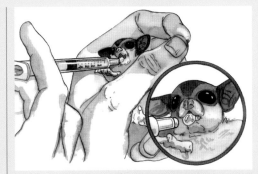

Offer the baby its milk formula one drop at a time.

the aquarium's top with plastic wrap. Leave enough air holes to allow for adequate ventilation. Make sure that the sides of the water containers are tall enough and smooth enough that the baby cannot climb up and fall into the water. Rewarm the water in the containers every couple of hours.

As the hand-reared baby matures, start offering it pureed fruits and vegetables and fruit juices. Gradually increase its repertoire of foods until it is eating an adult diet.

Stimulate the joey to urinate and defecate by gently stroking its cloacal aperture at the base of the tail with a moistened cotton swab.

Over the last few years, I've kept and bred several hundred sugar gliders. They make delightful pets that are easy to care for and, on the whole, have remarkably few health problems.

A pet glider that is fed a nutritious diet, kept clean and free of parasites, allowed sufficient exercise and stimulation, and not exposed to stressful or potentially harmful situations is likely to lead a long, healthy, and happy life.

Nutrition and Health

The importance of good nutrition in maintaining health cannot be stressed enough. Failure to provide nutritious foods in sensible amounts and combinations is *the* leading cause of ill health and premature death among pet gliders. The following are the most common nutritional disorders that affect sugar gliders.

Calcium Deficiency

While calcium deficiency occurs in only a

A healthy, bright-eyed, and alert juvenile glider.

minority of sugar gliders, it is their most common health problem. I have personally seen several cases of calcium deficiency among my own stock and have heard of numerous cases from other breeders and pet keepers around North America.

The signs associated with calcium deficiency are lameness, difficulty in moving across the wire of the cage, pelvic deformity, paralysis, and eventual death if left untreated. Most animals have a slow onset of symptoms, but when a bone is fractured due to poor calcification, observable signs such as lameness and paralysis may occur. The majority of sugar gliders that develop this complaint are adult females that are in the process of raising young. This is not really surprising when you consider that pregnancy, and especially lactation, makes extra demands on the body for calcium. However, male gliders are far from immune to the deficiencies associated with poor nutrition.

Sugar gliders develop calcium deficiency or metabolic bone disease (MBD) primarily because they are ingesting too much phosphorus in relation to their calcium intake. An overabundance of phosphorus in the diet interferes with calcium absorption. Other factors that decrease calcium absorption are vitamin D deficiency and excessive dietary fat. Vitamin D plays a role in controlling the absorption of calcium and its deposit in bones. Excessive fat can accumulate in the intestine where it combines with calcium to form insoluble soaps. These insoluble soaps are then excreted and the fat-bound calcium is lost.

When one looks at the nutritional content of the foods commonly fed to sugar gliders (see Nutritional Content of Common Sugar Glider Foods, page 55), it is easy to see why MBD is such a common problem. More than two-thirds of the fruits and vegetables listed have inverse ratios of calcium to phosphorus. In addition,

many of the protein rich foods such as red meat, poultry, eggs, insects, and nuts are deficient in calcium and high in fat.

To prevent your glider from developing calcium deficiency, emphasize calcium rich foods in its diet and judiciously ration foods that have inverse ratios of calcium and phosphorus and that are high in fat.

If you have an animal that you think may have MBD, consult your veterinarian. He or she can quite often confirm the diagnosis with X-rays because demineralized bones do not show up as well on an X-ray as healthy bones. Your veterinarian may choose to give an affected glider a series of calcium injections if it is not eating well and cannot take it in orally. The sick glider's diet should be adjusted accordingly and an oral calcium supplement provided once it gets back on its feet. However, your veterinarian is the most qualified person to select an appropriate course of treatment.

Don't give up on gliders that appear to be completely paralyzed. Even severely affected animals will often make a complete recovery with prompt and appropriate treatment.

Trimming Claws

Even after a sick glider gets back on its feet, it may be uncoordinated for a period of time. Before you put it back in a wire cage, trim its claws with a pair of small toenail clippers so it will be able to negotiate the wire more easily. Trimming claws is a two-person job, and leather gloves should be worn if the animal is not tame. Be careful to only take the very tip off of the claw. It will bleed if you take off too much.

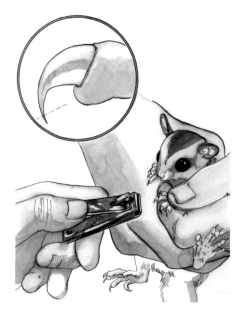

Be careful to only take the very tip off of the claw.

It is a good idea to routinely trim the claws of pet gliders because their sharp little claws can leave minute punctures in the skin of those handling them. The subcutaneous introduction of bacteria can result in dermatitis.

Obesity

Pet gliders that are allowed to overindulge in fat rich foods are quite likely to become obese, which can lead to a number of health problems including infertility, fat deposits in the eyes (calcified cholesterol deposits within the corneas, which can lead to blindness), lethargy, and a general decrease in life span. If your glider is gaining an excessive amount of weight, reduce the amount of fat in its diet by feeding less egg yolk, nuts, cheese, meat, and especially cat food.

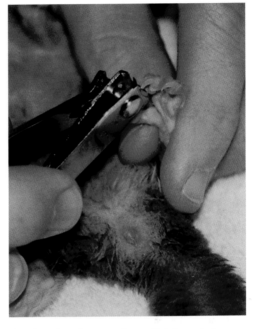

Emaciation

Sugar gliders can lose weight for a number of reasons including insufficient calories in the diet, malabsorption of nutrients, intestinal parasites, stress, and disease. Animals that are underweight or that are failing to grow should be taken to a veterinarian for assessment.

Constipation

Sugar gliders that do not consume enough roughage in their diet or that eat an excessive amount of dry cat food can develop constipation and become seriously ill or even die as a result. Constipated gliders often develop hard, distended abdomens and can be seen to strain in an exaggerated manner when they defecate. The resulting stools (if they do manage to pass anything) are often hard and dry. Once again, it is important to correct any obvious causalities in the glider's diet and to seek medical advice if the situation does not immediately remedy itself. Not only is constipation detrimental to health, but it is also an extremely uncomfortable situation for your pet to endure.

Diarrhea

Diarrhea can be caused by a number of factors, only one of which is improper diet. Diarrhea can be caused by an overindulgence in citrus fruits, lactose intolerance (which sometimes results when gliders are fed raw milk), and gastroenteritis. It can also be caused by stress and the ingestion of toxins.

Animals with persistent diarrhea can quickly become dangerously dehydrated. Gliders that have liquid diarrhea that lasts for more than 24 hours should be taken to a veterinarian for treatment. If there is blood in the stool the glider should be treated immediately.

Note: The ingestion of red and orange pigmented fruits and vegetables will sometimes result in stools that are orange-red in color, which can sometimes be mistaken for blood tinged stools.

The Importance of Hygiene

You cannot expect your pet to remain healthy if it is living in a dirty cage or eating and drinking from soiled dishes.

Spot clean your glider's cage once a day by washing any soiled surfaces. Special attention should be paid to areas where your pet tends to sit and eat. Food and water dishes must be kept scrupulously clean. Nesting material and cage-bottom material should be changed regularly. Toys and exercise wheels should be kept clean, and climbing branches should be replaced if they are soiled.

Once a week, remove your gliders from their cage in order to wash their entire enclosure with a solution of bleach and water. Once the cage has been rinsed to remove the bleach and it has completely dried, your pets can be returned to their home.

Hygiene is not only important to a pet's welfare but to its keeper's also, as there are diseases that can be passed from animals to humans. For instance, it is possible to contract salmonellosis from a pet that is infected with *Salmonella*. However, the likelihood of contracting an illness from your pet is remote especially if you follow some basic rules of hygiene:

• Always wash your hands with soap and water before and after handling a pet or cleaning its cage and dishes. Never handle a pet and then prepare food or handle infants without washing your hands first.

• Do not wash a pet's food and water receptacles, or its cage, in food preparation areas.

• What is common sense to an adult is not always obvious to a child. Teach children that they should not rub an animal against their face or allow an animal to lick their face. They should also be made aware that it is important to keep their hands out of their mouth, especially while they are handling pets. Emphasize the importance of hand washing and explain when and why it should be done. If the child is too young to follow hygienic precautions, then the child should not be allowed unsupervised access to the pet and its cage.

Parasites

Internal Parasites

These include roundworms, hookworms, and tapeworms. Infested animals often lose weight and have a coat that is dull and brittle. If you suspect that your glider may have internal parasites, take a sample of your pet's stools to your veterinarian for fecal analysis.

External Parasites

Common external parasites include ticks, mites, fleas, and lice.

Ivermectin that has been injected under the skin should take care of external as well as some (but by no means all) internal parasites. It is also important to thoroughly clean the treated animal's surroundings so that it will not be reinfested by contaminated bedding or wood shavings. Treat all animals in the same cage simultaneously along with any household pets that they come in contact with. You need not worry about catching fleas, lice, and so on, from your pets as parasites are host species-specific. Most animal parasites cannot live on humans for any length of time.

Pyrethin-based powders and sprays are supposed to be the safest topical treatment for external parasites, but I would hesitate to use them because they have an extremely strong odor that the sugar gliders might find distressing to their acute sense of smell. Your veterinarian is the most qualified person to make a decision about the appropriate method of parasite control based upon the specific type of pest and the severity of infestation. If you can, try to remove some of the offending insects from your pet's fur and stick them to a piece of adhesive tape for your veterinarian's perusal.

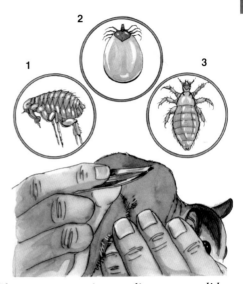

If you see a parasite crawling on your glider, try and remove it with a pair of tweezers. 1. Flea 2. Tick 3. Lice

Not all animals that repeatedly scratch at themselves do so because they have external parasites. Many animals, including sugar gliders, will scratch at themselves as part of their normal grooming routine. Unless you actually see critters crawling on your gliders or your veterinarian finds parasites in its stools, worming and delousing should not be necessary. To date, it has never been necessary to treat my gliders for parasites of any kind.

Bathing Gliders

An occasional bath is no guarantee that an animal will remain free of external parasites. Sugar gliders do not require bathing since they are very adept at grooming themselves and keep themselves very clean. However, I did once bathe a sugar glider that had fallen into a pitcher of apple juice. I felt compelled to bathe it after its

fur dried into stiff little spikes, but I only rinsed it with warm water and used no shampoo. I then placed the glider in an aquarium with a heating pad until it was completely dry. Don't try to blow dry your glider. The noise and the blast of hot air will scare the wits out of it.

Bathing a glider is much like bathing a cat— there's a lot of struggling and clawing involved. In general, it is neither necessary nor advisable to bathe sugar gliders.

Stress-Related Illness

All animals carry populations of internal and external bacteria. In a normal, healthy animal, the numbers of these bacteria are kept in check by the animal's immune system. When an animal becomes stressed, its immune system does not work as efficiently. Bacteria take the opportunity to proliferate and diseases can manifest themselves.

Stress can come from a variety of sources including illness, inadequate diet, unsanitary living conditions, stressful shipping conditions, an inadequate period of light and dark, a cage that is too small, overcrowding, overhandling, loneliness, boredom, excessive cold or heat, temperature fluctuations, inadequate ventilation, proximity to electrical appliances, terrorism by other household pets, and the list goes on.

The source of stress can be very difficult to pinpoint. What bothers one animal may not bother another at all. Stress also manifests itself in different ways. One animal might react to a stressful situation by ceasing to eat, while another might eat gluttonously. Where one animal reacts to stress by circling frantically in its cage, another might deal with the same situation by sleeping an excessive amount.

Stress and disease can form a chicken-and-egg relationship. Did the animal get sick because it was stressed or is it stressed because it is sick? Sometimes it is difficult to differentiate the cause from the effect, thus it is always best to consult your veterinarian if you have an animal that is exhibiting behavioral problems or clinical signs of illness.

Recognizing Ill Health

The common clinical signs of illness and injury include: open wounds; injuries and infections of the eyes that result in weeping, painful blinking, and hypersensitivity to light; a runny nose; vomiting; coughing; sneezing; noisy and difficult breathing; swellings; abscesses; red and scaly skin; balding, a dull coat; diarrhea; constipation; lameness; lack of coordination; paralysis; and weight loss.

Behavioral problems include: gluttonous eating; fasting; consumption of feces and bedding material; cannibalism of young; self-mutilation; frantic cage circling; habitual grooming that results in bald patches; and excessive sleeping.

Quarantine

An animal that is exhibiting behavioral problems or that has clinical signs of illness should be removed from the company of other animals in its cage. The quarantine cage or hospital cage for the sick animal should not be in proximity to the healthy animals. The cage containing the healthy animals should be thoroughly cleaned to remove any pathogens.

The Hospital Cage

Aquariums make ideal hospital cages. They are easy to keep clean and the sick animal is sheltered from drafts and doesn't have to struggle to negotiate cage wire in its weakened state. A heating pad set on *low* can be placed under the floor of the aquarium if the animal has a tendency to become chilled and torpid without an external source of heat. If the animal is so sick that it cannot move around, it is important to turn it frequently and to check underneath its body to make sure that the floor of the aquarium is not getting too hot. Your veterinarian will give you specific instructions depending on your pet's condition.

Finding a Veterinarian

Do not assume that any one of your local veterinarians will see your ill sugar glider. Not all veterinarians are prepared to treat exotic pets. It is a good idea to locate a willing veterinarian prior to a medical emergency arising or, preferably, before you acquire your sugar glider.

If you buy your sugar glider locally, it is quite likely that the breeder or pet shop owner will be able to provide you with the name of the veterinarian that they consult.

UNDERSTANDING SUGAR GLIDERS

Sugar gliders express themselves quite eloquently through body language, behavior, and vocalizations. It won't take you long to figure out what your glider is trying to say.

Sugar Gliders in the Wild

Habitat

Sugar gliders are found in the forests of northeast, east, and southeast Australia and Papua-New Guinea as well as in some of the islands in the Indonesian chain. They have also been successfully introduced into Tasmania.

Diet in the Wild

Sugar glider colonies spend their days curled up in a companionable ball in the hollow of a tree trunk. When night falls they emerge from their lair to look for their favorite foods. As their name suggests, sugar gliders have a preference for sweet foods. One of their favorite native treats is the sweet sap of the wattle or acacia gum. Sugar gliders will travel some

This glider looks like it is ready to play "catch me if you can."

distance in search of the sap of this particular tree. Once a sap feeding site has been staked out by the group, they will vigorously defend it by biting and chasing away trespassers. They are also quite fond of a certain species of Eucalyptus that has a sweet, carbohydrate-rich sap. The protein in their omnivorous diet is provided by insects, birds eggs, and small vertebrates such as small birds, rodents, and lizards.

Gliding

The sugar glider travels through the midnight treetops by leaping acrobatically from branch to branch or, where the distance is too great to jump, it leaps into the air and unfolds its sails of skin to glide up to several hundred feet. The tail is used like a rudder to control the direction of flight.

Sugar gliders usually glide from the top of one tree to the base of another. At the end

The sugar glider can glide several hundred feet through the air.

unrelated adults of both sexes, and several generations of offspring.

Sugar gliders correlate their mating season to periods of insect abundance, suggesting that they need the extra protein in order to breed. The most dominant male breeds most, if not all, of the females within his group. Because the dominant males are usually the fittest of the males, this ensures that the babies will have the best available genes imparted to them. Most of the glider family are promiscuous and one dominant male will usually completely monopolize the breeding within his group. The exception to this is Leadbeater's possum, which is the only member of the glider family that forms monogamous pairs.

of the glide, just before touch down, the glider makes a last second upward swoop, which slows its descent and lessens the impact. However, slow motion photography has shown these landings to be far from the soft and graceful landing that the naked eye perceives. Only the animal's sharp grasping claws prevent it from ricocheting off into the underbrush. It makes one wonder how a little glider in its mother's pouch survives all the jostling and thumping!

For all their gliding prowess, sugar gliders would not win the gold in the gliding Olympics. That honor would go to the flying lemur of the Philippines and Southeast Asia that can make glides of 445 feet or more.

Mating in the Wild

Sugar gliders are highly social animals that colonize in groups of up to 12 individuals. These groups typically contain up to four

Vocalizations

In addition to scent gland communication, sugar gliders communicate and make their feelings known through a series of vocalizations:

Barking: Short muted barks that sound rather like a small dog barking in the distance help them to keep tabs on each other's position.

Sneezing: When members of the same group disagree (more often than not over food), they make a sneezing sound that translates into "go away, I saw it first."

Hissing: Dependent gliders will sometimes make a low hissing sound. This sound is meant to communicate distress and will bring other members of the group running to its aid. Babies also make this noise when hungry.

Crabbing: By far their most extraordinary vocalization is the one they make when disturbed in their nest. It defies description but sounds a little like one of those crank handled rattles that are popular at New Year parties.

I have heard this noise described as "crabbing." The noise is surprisingly loud and threatening considering that it is being emitted by such a small and harmless creature. This noise is produced to communicate displeasure or fear. A pet glider sometimes makes this noise when it is disturbed from sleep but usually stops once it recognizes the scent of the person picking it up.

Body Language and Behavior

Besides scent gland and vocal communication, sugar gliders are also able to communicate certain moods and intentions through body language and behavior.

The Defensive Glider

A sugar glider that feels threatened often takes up a defensive posture. You may see this posture if you reach toward a glider that isn't quite sure about you and your intentions. Typically the animal will stand up on its hind legs with its head extended forward and the mouth open and tilted upward to show off its teeth. The front feet are raised up in a fending-off gesture. As a variation of this, the animal might lie on its back with all four feet extended towards a perceived threat. This posture is almost always accompanied by a crabbing vocalization.

If your pet glider takes up this posture when you reach for it, offer it the heel of your hand to sniff. If the glider does panic and attempt to bite, the flat

heel of your hand is less likely to sustain a penetrating bite than the more vulnerable, thin skinned, and sensitive tips of your fingers. Once the glider has recognized your scent and settled down, you can scoop it into the palm of your hand and cup it against your body.

The Depressed or Sick Glider

Sugar gliders that are kept singly and have little or no interaction with a human companion often become depressed. Nontame gliders should always be kept in pairs or groups because they are not likely to be handled. Likewise, if you find that you can't handle your tame glider on a regular basis, acquire a companion for it. Depressed gliders often sleep an excessive amount (most of the night as well as the day) and as a result will not eat very much and may suffer from malnutrition. Typically, a depressed animal will lay its ears flat against its head and have a generally miserable expression. If you have a lone sugar glider that meets this description, take it to your veterinarian to evaluate any health-related reasons for its behavior. If it is physically healthy and increasing the amount of handling it receives produces no improvement in its demeanor, look for a companion animal to keep it company.

If your glider is not sure about you and your intentions, it may take up this posture when you reach for it.

The Neurotic Glider

Animals that are unhappy due to a cage that is too small or boredom or stress sometimes behave neurotically. They may frantically circle in their cage or repeat the same motion or path over and over again as if they have been automated. In extreme cases they may even self-mutilate by chewing their tail or a limb, or by grooming themselves bald. If your pet is behaving this way, take it to your veterinarian to eliminate any medical reasons for its behavior. If the glider is kept singly, try and increase the amount of time you spend handling it. Provide it with a larger cage and a bigger variety of toys, hiding places, and distractions. Once again, if these measures fail to produce an improvement in your pet's behavior, consider looking for a companion animal to keep it company.

The Playful Glider

Sugar gliders that are feeling particularly mischievous and playful often make short little hops from side to side as they run along, sometimes doing a complete 180 degree turn in the air before landing back on their feet. My gliders like to play "catch me if you can" by running up the back of the couch toward me and then hopping back and running away.

Natural Enemies

In the wild, sugar gliders live about seven or eight years at most. Few will enjoy the luxury of growing old and dying in their sleep, for the gliders share their environment with several enemies. Chief among them is, as always, humankind, which destroys their natural habitat by clearing forests for agricultural use. Sugarcane farming in Australia has had a

significant impact on several types of gliders. The mahogany glider was described in 1893 and was not officially seen for the next 103 years. During this time, some 80 percent of its habitat was cleared for agriculture. The mahogany glider is now confined to an area of only 81 miles (130 kilometers) long by some 3–6 miles (5–10 kilometers) wide. It is hardly surprising that they are considered an endangered species.

Besides human beings, the sugar glider's chief enemies are primarily birds of prey, particularly the barking or winking owl and the powerful owl, and arboreal snakes, such as carpet pythons.

Scent Marking

Sugar gliders maintain group cohesion and identity by constantly reintroducing themselves. Their version of shaking hands requires that the female rub the top of her head on the male's scent gland. A male in turn says "How do you do?" by rubbing his head gland and chest gland on the female's chest and cloacal area. It is primarily by this means that gliders identify themselves and recognize those around them as each glider has a slightly different scent "signature." Males mark their territory by dragging their scent glands across branches. Strange sugar gliders that stray into the group's territory are viciously attacked and bitten.

INFORMATION

Clubs and Associations

The International Sugar Glider Association (ISGA)
www.isga.org

Products

Supplier of Biolac
www.peeweespamperedpetproducts.com

Supplier of Gliderade
Exotic Nutrition Pet Co.
737 Industrial Park Drive
Newport News, VA 23608
Phone: (866) 988-0301
Fax: (757) 988-0321
www.exoticnutrition.com

Safety Wheels
Wodent Wheels
www.transoniq.com

Safety Wheel Insert
Suncoast Sugar Gliders
Phone: (727) 343-8577
www.sugar-gliders.com

Supplier of Nekton-Lori
Phone: (520) 323-9912
www.centralah.com

Rep-Cal Calcium with Vit. D_3
Rep-Cal Research Labs
Los Gatos, CA 95031
Phone: (800) 406-6446
www.repcal.com

Reptivite
Zoo Med Laboratories
San Luis Obispo, CA 93401
Phone: (888) 496-6633
www.zoomed.com

Scenic Bird Food (Psittacine Diet)
Marion Zoological, Inc.
2003 E. Center Circle
Plymouth, MN 55441
Phone: (800) 327-7974
www.scenicbirdfood.com

Supplier of Vionate Vitamin Mineral Powder
The Gliding Room
2400 Keene Park Drive
Largo, FL 33771
Phone: (727) 535-9419
www.sugarglider63.com

Further Reading

Balch, J. F., MD, and P. A. Balch, CNC. *Prescription for Nutritional Healing.* New York: Avery Publishing Group, Inc., 1990.

Breeden, Stanley and Kay. *Living Marsupials.* Australia: William Collins Ltd., 1970.

Fowler, Murray E., DVM. *Zoo & Wild Animal Medicine: Current Therapy 3.* Philadelphia: W. B. Saunders Company, 1993.

Gallerstein, Gary A., DVM. *The Complete Bird Owner's Handbook.* New York: Howell Book House, 1994.

Macdonald, David, Dr. *The Encyclopedia of Mammals.* New York: Facts on File Inc., 1987.

MacPherson, Caroline. *Keeping and Breeding Sugar Gliders as Pets.* Caroline MacPherson, 1990.

Netzer, Corinne T. *The Corinne T. Netzer Encyclopedia of Food Values.* New York: Dell Publishing, 1992.

Raven and Johnson. *Biology.* Times Mirror/Mosby College Publishing, 1986.

Smith, A. P. and I. D. Hume. *Possums and Gliders.* Sydney: Australian Mammal Society, 1984.

Strahan, R. *The Mammals of Australia.* Sydney: Reed Books, 1995.

Williams, Sue Rodwell. *Essentials of Nutrition and Diet Therapy.* St. Louis: Times Mirror/ Mosby Publishing, 1986.

Hobbyist Magazine

Rare Breeds Journal

A bimonthly magazine that has a special section called Jumping Pouches, which often features informative articles about sugar gliders and other marsupials.

P.O. Box 66

Crawford, NE 69339

Phone: (308) 665-1431

Fax: (308) 665-3919

www.rarebreedsjournal.com

Useful Addresses

Caroline Wightman

Fax: (250) 766-4162

E-mail: pygmypets@shaw.ca

www.pygmypets.com

Sugar glider information and supplies.

United States Department of Agriculture Headquarters

USDA/APHIS/AC

4700 River Road, Unit 84

Riverdale, MD 20737-1234

Phone: (301) 734-7833

Fax: (301) 734-4978

www.aphis.usda.gov

GLOSSARY

Arboreal Living in trees.

Diprodonts Animals that have only two lower incisors, which are usually large and forward pointing.

Embryonic The early developmental stage of an animal produced from a fertilized egg.

Estrus A period during which the female is sexually receptive. Associated with ovulation of the egg.

Marsupial Unlike placental mammals, marsupial mammals reproduce in such a way that little or no emphasis is placed on placentally gestating their young. Instead, marsupials give birth to rudimentary offspring that mature in a pouch on the mother's abdomen. Within

the pouch there are nipples that the offspring attaches to. Lactation rather than gestation is emphasized in marsupial reproduction.

Nocturnal Active at night.

Opposable The ability to bring the thumb or big toe into contact with the other digits in a grasping action, thus enabling objects to be picked up, gripped, and held.

Ovary The organ in which eggs are produced.

Ovulation The release of an egg or eggs from the ovary.

Patagium A gliding membrane typically stretching down the sides of the body between the forelimbs and hindlimbs and sometimes including the tail. Found in flying squirrels, bats, sugar gliders, and so on.

Placental Mammal A placenta is a structure that connects the developing baby and the mother's womb to ensure a supply of nutrients to the fetus and removal of its waste products. Only placental mammals have a well-developed placenta. Marsupials have a rudimentary placenta, or none at all.

Prehensile From the Latin, *prehendere*, to seize. Adapted for grasping.

Syndactylous Pertaining to the second and third toes of some mammals, which are joined together so that they appear to be a single toe with a split nail. In kangaroos and sugar gliders, these syndactylous toes are used as a fur comb.

Torpor Lethargy.

Uterus In mammals, a chamber in which the developing embryo is contained and nurtured during pregnancy.

Vaginae Plural of vagina. Female accessory reproductive organ that receives sperm from the male penis; forms part of the birth canal.

I N D E X

About the Author

Caroline Wightman works as an ambulance paramedic in her hometown of Winfield in British Columbia, Canada. Prior to becoming a paramedic, she worked part-time for a veterinarian and completed her pre-veterinary medicine course in Grande Prairie, Alberta. She currently raises a variety of exotic animals on her small farm and writes articles for several exotic animal magazines.

Acknowledgments

Special thanks to Steven Jackson, who is currently writing his Ph.D. thesis on the sociobiology of the Mahogany glider in Australia, for all his invaluable information regarding gliders in general. Thanks also to Dr. Darcy Rae, DVM of the Tri Lake Animal Clinic, for his unfailing support and patience in treating my strange collection of animals.

Cover Photos

Front cover, inside front cover, inside back cover, back cover: McDonald Wildlife.

Photo Credits

All interior photos by the author except for Isabelle Francais: pp. 3, 4, 5, 7, 9, 11, 13, 14, 15, 17, 18, 20, 22, 31, 34, 42, 44, 46, 48, 50, 57, 58, 60, 61, 62, 76, 77, 85; McDonald Wildlife: pp. 6, 10, 84, 89, 93; Punchstock: p. 92; Shutterstock: p. 16.

All inquiries should be addressed to:
Barron's Educational Series, Inc.
250 Wireless Boulevard
Hauppauge, NY 11788
www.barronseduc.com

ISBN-13: 978-0-7641-3768-6
ISBN-10: 0-7641-3768-9

Library of Congress Catalog Card No. 2007037819

Library of Congress Cataloging-in-Publication Data
Wightman, Caroline.
    Sugar gliders : everything about purchase, care, nutrition, behavior, and breeding / Caroline Wightman— 2nd ed.
        p. cm. — (A complete pet owner's manual)
    Includes index.
    ISBN-13: 978-0-7641-3768-6 (alk. paper)
    ISBN-10: 0-7641-3768-9 (alk. paper)
    1. Sugar gliders as pets. I. Title.

    SF459.S83W54 2007
    636.92'3–dc22   2007037819

Printed in China
9 8 7 6 5 4 3 2 1